From Mom + Dad
1978

Rowland Hilder

ROWLAND HILDER
Painter and Illustrator

John Lewis

BARRIE & JENKINS
COMMUNICA - EUROPA

TO EDITH HILDER

Text © John Noel Claude Lewis 1978
Illustrations © Rowland Hilder

First published in 1978
by Barrie & Jenkins Ltd
24 Highbury Crescent, London N5 1RX

ISBN 0 214 20425 1

AUTHOR'S NOTE

My thanks are due to Rowland Hilder for his unstinted help
over the writing and production of this book. Also to his family
for their affectionate co-operation and particularly to the
artist's son-in-law Rado Klose, for the trouble and care he has
bestowed on photographing every painting, sketch and
drawing shown here.

Finally, and this is becoming something of a habit in my books,
my gratitude to my wife Griselda who has helped me in endless
ways.

Printed in England by Shenval Press Ltd, London and Harlow

Contents

List of illustrations

1922 Pencil drawing of a sailing barge at anchor off Greenwich. $10\frac{1}{4} \times 12$in

Part I

1. The beginnings: paintings and drawings on the river Thames

'One of my first and most lasting memories is being taken by my father from Long Island, where we lived, over to Manhattan. It was a cold autumn day but the sun was shining. We walked down to Battery Point and stood looking across the water. We were looking into the sun and the water was speckled with light. I think it was that sight that made me want to paint. I can see it still.'

Rowland Hilder was born in 1905 at Great Neck, Long Island, which was the home of the US Merchant Marine Academy. His parents were British, but his father, because of some disagreement with Rowland's grandfather, and also maybe through a spirit of adventure, had crossed the Atlantic and settled in Long Island with his newly wedded wife. Later they moved to an apartment in New York near Central Park and finally settled in Morristown, New Jersey. Here Rowland went to school. In most years he and his mother and father came back to England in the summer to visit his grandparents who lived at Birling in Kent. He recalled their final return to England. 'Early in 1915 my father (who was also christened Roland though without the 'w') thought that the British Army was not doing too well on the Western Front, so he decided he had better come to their help. We travelled back to England in the *Lusitania* on the last trip she made before she was torpedoed and sunk by the German U-boats. I can remember that she was painted black all over and that blankets were hung over the portholes at night.'

Roland Hilder senior joined the Royal Horse Artillery and as a form of insurance against the likelihood of his being killed, he bought his wife a tobacconist's shop in the New Cross Road. Why he chose New Cross and why a tobacconist's shop, his son never discovered. In due course, however, Mr Hilder did return and they continued to live in New Cross. In 1918 Rowland was sent to Aske's Hatcham School. He was a tall gangling boy and was placed in a higher form than he should have been. 'Put there', he said, 'because of my size, not my intellect.' He was miserable at school. He could not spell, so he spent his time drawing pictures and he spoke with a broad American accent, which endeared him neither to his masters nor to his fellow schoolboys.

The only encouragement he received at Aske's was from 'Beak' Smith-Collins, the art master, a kindly man so nicknamed because of the size of his nose. Smith-Collins saw the potential not only in the sketches of the riverside that the young Hilder was doing, but even more in the boy's dedication to drawing. It was ultimately Smith-Collins who made it clear to his parents that he should take up art as a career.

New Cross, as far as Rowland was concerned, had few things to be

1920 Pen and indian ink drawing of a lighter on the Thames made before Rowland Hilder entered Goldsmith's College School of Art. It was this drawing that made the Principal suggest he might be a suitable pupil for the etching class. 6 × 6¼in

1921 Early pen drawing done before coming under the influence of Edmund J. Sullivan. 6 × 7in

1921 Pen drawing of shipping: an attempt at drawing for reproduction. 4 × 6in

said for it. It was however near the river Thames. New Cross is bordered on one side by Deptford and the Surrey Docks and on the other by Greenwich and Wren's Naval College. Beyond Greenwich is Woolwich with its shipyards where in the early 1920s, as well as building ships, they were still breaking up the old 'wooden walls'. In those days on the Woolwich waterfront the atmosphere was filled with the smell of Stockholm tar and the noise of riveters, caulking mallets and the hammering of the ship breakers. Upstream Scandinavian timber barques were unloading in Deptford Creek and great grain ships lay at moorings in Limehouse Reach as their cargoes were shifted into lighters. Rowland spent all his spare time drawing on the waterside. But the hours he spent in Aske's school rooms were unmitigated misery.

There was a small paint factory across the road from where the Hilders lived. Over the entrance a board announced 'W. H. Screeton Paintmaker'. Bill Screeton, the founder of the firm, was a character much larger than life and a raconteur of Dickensian stature. He had a profound influence not only on Rowland Hilder but on a number of other students from Goldsmith's. He was a philosopher, counsellor and universal provider. He had been born in Hull and had come up to London looking for work whilst he was still in his teens. He had ridden from Yorkshire on a bicycle and was pedalling southwards down the Peckham Road when he saw some men unloading a furnace boiler outside a theatre. They were making heavy weather of this job, so he dismounted from his bike and went over to see if they needed any help. Within a minute or so they had handed the job over to him. With levers, chocks and ropes he soon had the boiler off the cart and moved into the theatre's furnace room. The theatre manager who had been standing by observing this performance called him over.

'I've been watching you. What training have you had?'
'I was apprenticed to the Post Office as an engineer and electrician.'
'Do you want a job?' the manager asked.
'Yes, that's why I've come up here.'
'You've got one. Start right away.'

So young Bill Screeton started work in the theatre. He revelled in the life. All the stage hands were ex-navy or ex-merchant seamen. He learned much from them. He helped to install electric lighting and he was probably the first man to use coloured gells and the first man to show a sunset on a London stage. He became friends with scene painters and artists. He was loaned to the Lyceum Theatre for a year and did the lighting for at least one of Henry Irving's productions and all the time he was educating himself. From his contact with artists he became involved in paint making. In

1922 'Stumpy barge'. One of Rowland Hilder's first etchings. 2¾ × 3¾in

1928 Screeton's caravan at High Halstow. Watercolour drawing

partnership with a man called Zoffel he marketed the first
cellulose paint under the name of Domilac. Finally he set up his
own little paint factory in the New Cross Road and there he made
very high quality oil paints. As a result of this he had a close
connection with various art schools including Goldsmith's. He
provided Clive Gardiner, who was later to be Principal of
Goldsmith's, with paint for the murals that Gardiner, helped by
Hilder and various other students, painted for the Wembley
Empire Exhibition in 1923.

Bill Screeton had a caravan at Allhallows on the Isle of Grain,
which lies between the mouths of the rivers Thames and Medway.
He used to invite students there for the weekends. There they
camped and sailed and went for great long walks. They sketched
and they talked far into the night. The conversation was
dominated by this wise and witty man. Bill Screeton opened up
new horizons for all of them. His acolytes said he was like a
one-man university.

Rowland Hilder was already drawing in pen and ink and his work
was showing his interest in the effects of light and shade. The pen
sketch shown here of lighters with shipping in the background
drawn against the light is an Impressionist drawing. It was done
when he was fifteen and led Frederick Marriott, the Principal of
Goldsmith's College School of Art, to recommend that he should in
due course enter the etching class at Goldsmith's.

1921 Pencil drawing of a collier at Greenwich
Power Station. $11 \times 8\frac{1}{4}$ in

c.1927 Drawing made in Sullivan's life class, where the students were told to draw the whole scene instead of just the model. They were encouraged to 'compose' the material into a rectangle and so to tell a story, or at least make a comment on the situation. $9\frac{3}{4} \times 7\frac{1}{2}$in

Even the worst of days come to an end. In 1921, at the age of sixteen, Hilder left Aske's and was admitted to Goldsmith's. It must have seemed to him as if the gates of Heaven had opened.

When Rowland Hilder entered Goldsmith's the reverberations not only of the war to end wars but also of Roger Fry's two pre-war Post-Impressionist Exhibitions were still rumbling round the London art scene. Roger Fry was holding his position as a powerful influence, at least over the London Group. Clive Bell was laying down the law about what modern painting was all about, and that seemed to be summed up in one word – Cézanne, coupled with what Lord Clark has called 'that catchpenny phrase, significant form'. The brothers Nash, amongst the younger men,

were at the front of this movement, with Paul Nash the more
eloquent, though John Nash was carving his own particular niche
in landscape painting without taking much notice of all this windy
talk. Sickert had not yet returned to London from Dieppe, Spenser
Gore and Harold Gilman had both died and Camden Town was not
what it was. Augustus John was not in the Royal Academy, but
Lavery and Orpen were. And there were other scenes. One of the
more thriving was the 'etching boom'. Frank Brangwyn and
W. L. Wyllie were the artists of this movement that appealed most
to Hilder. They both drew ships. Brangwyn was thought by the
etching purists to be debasing the medium by his use of huge zinc
plates and the fact that every print he took was different from the
last. They derisively called him 'a poor man's Piranesi'. It was F. L.
Griggs who won their approval. Griggs had the additional credit of
having rediscovered Samuel Palmer. Hilder, as a result of his
watery bent, had only one other god at that time and that was
James McNeill Whistler.

At Goldsmith's and at home in New Cross above the tobacconist's
shop Rowland Hilder lived, slept and dreamt drawing. He was
fortunate in his choice of art school, for Goldsmith's had an
established reputation for fine draughtmanship. Hilder was
placed, as Marriott had suggested when he went up for his
interview, in the etching class. First under Marriott himself and
then under a very talented young man called Alfred Bentley.
Unhappily, very soon after Hilder's arrival at Goldsmith's,
Bentley died quite suddenly from pneumonia.

Goldsmith's School of Art was in the same building as the London
University Teacher Training College. It was one of the only two
art schools that were part of London University (the other was the
Slade). The building had once housed the Royal Naval Hospital
School which is now at Holbrook in Suffolk. The art school was on
the first and second floors of this rather forbidding building. One
approaches it through long and echoing corridors and then up
stone staircases enclosed in a steel cage like a prison. Once inside
the art school itself, the atmosphere changes. It is a cheerful,
spacious and colourful place.

Even in his first year at Goldsmith's, Hilder was spending every
moment he could on the waterfront, particularly when he should
have been drawing from the antique. The drawing of the stern of a
collier aground at low water alongside the unloading staithes
gives some indication of his developing powers of
draughtsmanship. In these early etchings and pen drawings of
steamers and sailing barges, he made much use of cross-hatching
for the tones. His style was quite unformed, yet these are more than
a promising student's drawings.

1926 'The tug'. Etching $6\frac{7}{8} \times 9$in

In the etching class at Goldsmith's, Bentley was succeeded by Malcolm Osborne, who was an ARA with a considerable reputation. Osborne immediately took an interest in Hilder and urged him to stick to etching, which, so Osborne suggested, would be a sinecure for his election in due course to the Royal Academy. However, it was not to be.

Rowland Hilder did not stay the course as an etcher mainly, so he says, because he could not stand the smell of the acid! This was a fortunate disability in more ways than one. The so-called 'etching boom' was coming to an end. He was moved from the etching class into the illustration class where he came under the spell of Edmund J. Sullivan.

Sullivan was a remarkable teacher, as well as being a very fine pen draughtsman. Some years later Clive Gardiner, who succeeded Marriott as Principal of Goldsmith's said: 'Whenever I am with Sullivan, I get the impression of being with a *very great* man.'

Sullivan certainly had a presence. When he was younger he was often mistaken for Mr Asquith, the Liberal Prime Minister. He used to walk in Hyde Park for the pleasure and the amusement of this mistaken identity and of returning the salutes of people as they took off their hats to him. Sullivan had been great friends with Phil May and Tom Browne. Their joint capacity for strong drink appeared unlimited. Unfortunately it was not and both Phil

1922 Influences: pen drawing by Edmund J. Sullivan of a man's head from his book *Line*, published by Chapman and Hall

May and Tom Browne died before they were forty. Sullivan, who was Irish, must have had a copper-bottomed stomach for he lived until he was seventy. With all of that he was a kind man, with an ability to see the good points in a student's drawing. His method of teaching was to discover just what motivated or excited students and then to build up their confidence on that.

'He had a knack of unmasking your great and sometimes secret aspirations', Rowland remarked. He also kept the students drawing in their sketch-books, in the street, in the buses and trams, on the underground railway and above all in pubs (of which Rowland's parents did not approve). In the life class, he would sometimes make the students turn their backs on the model and draw each other. Sullivan encouraged the students to compose material within the confines of a rectangle and then either to make the drawing tell a story or at least make a comment on the situation. He breathed life into the life class and turned it away from being an often meaningless academic exercise into what was really an illustration class. Sickert supported this view when he said: 'We must try to pose, so to light and so to "cut" the nude so that the student can forget the lifeless formula of generations of ushers, and see what creative artists have ever seen in the nude.'

When talking about Sullivan, Rowland Hilder said: 'I remember once in the old litho room, it was a summer afternoon, the windows were open and a cricket match was going on below. There was the

1924 Flushing. Watercolour and carbon pencil drawing 14 × 20in

noise of a bat hitting a ball. Sullivan looked up from my drawing
and said: "You hear that crack of bat and ball? You get an
impression of what has happened – you paint that impression." He
then went on to talk about Expressionist painting: "You get cross,
your paint brush or your pen splutters and blots. That is part of
your expression and that is what Expressionism is all about – of
making use of the element of chance, of the happy accident." about
line drawing, Sullivan said: "A single line can express vitality,
like the single note of a violin." ' In addition to these aphorisms he
was feeding Hilder with examples of the work of all the great
draughtsmen of the past – Holbein, Dürer, Ingres, Rembrandt and
some lesser and later ones like Boyd Houghton, Aubrey Beardsley
and Augustus John. Of all these Dürer was the one who at that
time made the greatest impression on Rowland Hilder's work. This
was heady stuff for a young man.

It was during Rowland's second year at Goldsmith's that
Sullivan's illustrated edition of Tennyson's *Maud* was published.
These illustrations in their romantic freedom were a great
advance on the Düreresque drawings that Sullivan had done for
Carlyle's *Sartor Resartus* some twenty years earlier. The drawings
for *Maud* had a marked effect on Rowland Hilder's pen drawing.

The other artists who had most influence on Hilder in those early
Goldsmith's days after he had left the etching class were Muirhead
Bone and Frank Brangwyn. Bone was a fine draughtsman,
particularly of architecture, who often worked with a conté pencil,
a medium that Hilder was soon to find useful. Brangwyn had an
even greater influence on the young man.

It is worth while pausing for a moment to consider this artist, who
at that time was probably the only British artist whose name was
well known abroad, known even as far away as Tokyo. Brangwyn
had been born in Bruges, the son of a Welsh architect who gave
him such schooling as he had. He came to London and worked for
three years in William Morris's workshops in Oxford Street, doing
facsimiles of Flemish tapestries. This spell of drudgery was
interspersed with bouts of foreign travel, for he had fallen in love
with the sea. A painting called *The Buccaneers* exhibited in 1893
(at the Salon) created a sensation in France. He was a romantic of
romantics. James Laver wrote in 1956 in Brangwyn's obituary
notice in *The Times*: 'He loved the sweeping arches of a bridge,
sheer walls, immense girders, ships towering upwards like the edge
of a cliff and railway stations like deep caverns belching smoke.'

In 1904 Brangwyn did an etching of shipbreaking at Woolwich
Dockyard, called *Breaking up the Hannibal.* The marked
chiaroscuro with inky black shadows and strong highlights

1916 Influences: pen drawing by Frank Brangwyn of the docks at
Antwerp from *Belgium* by Hugh Stokes, published by Kegan Paul, 1916

foreshadowed much of Rowland Hilder's early work, as did the
lithograph of London showing St Paul's against the setting sun
with radiating beams of light. Rowland Hilder can remember how
an older student at Goldsmith's (his name was Graham
Sutherland) gave him a long talk on the virtues of Brangwyn's
etchings.

Now Brangwyn's use of black would not have been approved of by
the Impressionists, as Hilder remarked, 'Black in paintings was
virtually "blacked" by them.' For instance John Nash recalls how
Harold Gilman had told him in no uncertain terms never to use

1917 Influences: men of the Royal Field Artillery cleaning their guns.
Conté pencil and watercolour drawing by Muirhead Bone from *The
Western Front*. Published by Newnes

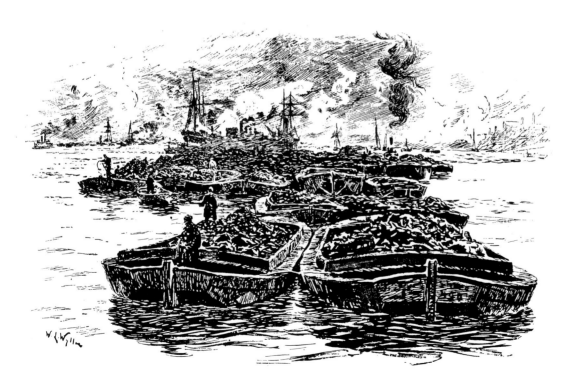

1896 Influences: Lighters on the Thames. Pen drawing by W. L. Wyllie

pure black, but to make it up from other colours. 'As I grow older', Nash remarked not long before he died, 'I found that a bit of a nonsense. Ivory black is a lovely colour, full of sepia tones. Even lamp black, the coldest and blackest of black has its place.' There are plenty of other illustrious precedents for the use of black amongst the modern painters including Picasso, and Rouault.

The use of black has played an important part in Hilder's development as a painter, as has the use of counter-change, an essential ingredient in any old master composition. There are, after all, other sources for graphic expression and other ways of painting than the methods developed by the Impressionists and those that followed them. For instance, Lovat Fraser, an artist who, when Rowland Hilder first entered Goldsmith's, had only just died, made a brilliant use of the blocking-in process which he learned from looking at Rembrandt's paintings. With the use of a reed pen and indian ink, Lovat Fraser blocked in his little decorations to children's books and then filled in the white areas with brilliant colour. It was comparable to the glazing and the leading of a stained glass window. All this and much else was grist to young Hilder's mill.

These romantic influences were quite outside the modern movement. At Goldsmith's most of the students were belated followers of the Camden Town Impressionists and some in the etching class, like Graham Sutherland who was influenced by Paul Nash, were breaking away from following Samuel Palmer to work in a more contemporary idiom. None of this modern movement was any help to Hilder who, at that stage, was hell-bent on becoming a marine painter. If you wanted to paint ships, he felt you had to spend all your time in getting to know about them, in sailing in them and in drawing them. And draw them he did, not only from the waterside but also from the thwarts of a small sailing dinghy which he used to hire from an old man in Bugsby's Reach. The fee for a day's hiring was one shilling and sixpence. He also made many sketching trips in the *Royal Eagle,* an old paddle steamer that used to ply between Tower Bridge, Southend and Margate. Many years later he did a painting of her steaming up Sea Reach. It appeared in a series of advertisements for Shell on the theme of industrial archaeology.

In 1924 Hilder won a travelling scholarship sponsored by Cadbury's for decorating the top of a chocolate box. For this he did an ambitious line drawing of an old sailing ship and won the first prize of £50. *The Times* art critic in a review of the exhibition of the designs for this competition, which was held at the Victoria and Albert Museum, wrote: 'Time was when "chocolate box" was a term of artistic reproach; nowadays we invite the flower of our art

1519 Influences: 'St Anthony' before the town. Steel engraving by
Albrecht Dürer. The town is Nuremberg

schools to apply their talents and training to chocolate box
decoration. The Cadbury Bournville travelling scholarship has
been given to Mr Rowland Frederick Hilder of Goldsmith's for a
black-and-white design for a poster, press illustration and box lid.'
This was Rowland Hilder's first modest step to fame.

Hilder's idea of seeing the Continent was not to go to Paris, the
centre of the modern art movement, or to Florence to study the
paintings of the Renaissance; instead he went to the Low
Countries and, to eke out his £50, he signed on to a small coaster as
purser and sailed to Antwerp and on to Brussels.

His reasons for going to the Netherlands were simple enough for a
would-be marine painter. The Dutch were after all the great
marine painters and the fishing boats of Zeeland and the Zuider
Zee were still as they were in the seventeenth century; and if that
was not enough – Rembrandt came from Amsterdam and Dürer had
thought the Low Countries worth a prolonged visit.

The Bo'sun. $5\frac{3}{4} \times 2\frac{1}{2}$ in

The Chief Engineer. $6\frac{1}{2} \times 6$ in

Pencil portraits drawn whilst crossing the North Sea to Holland and Belgium in the summer of 1924.

The Captain on the bridge. $4\frac{3}{4} \times 3\frac{1}{4}$ in

The First Mate. $5\frac{1}{4} \times 5\frac{1}{4}$ in

1924 Pencil and wash drawing of the deck of the steamer. $9 \times 11\frac{1}{2}$in

On the North Sea crossing to Antwerp, Hilder made drawings of the steamer and her equipment and drew portraits of the skipper, the engineer, the mate and the bosun. When they arrived in the Scheldt, he did another drawing of the Customs Officer, a sad-eyed walrus-moustached old man. As well as all this his sketch-book was filled with notes of shipping and the low sky lines of Flushing, Antwerp and the Scheldt.

The ship entered the Canal Maritime de Bruxelles au Rupel and steamed slowly up to Brussels, docking in one of the basins on the outskirts of the city. For a day or so, Hilder stayed on board the ship, nervously resisting the crew's invitations to visit the local brothels. When their importunities became too pressing, he went off on his own. He took a train to Flushing, then by bus crossed to the north of the island of Walcheren passing through Middelburg on his way to the little fishing town of Veere. He fell in love with this beautiful place. He drew the fishing boats, the aaken and the botters, and the old houses, the great lump of the cathedral and the

The Customs Officer in the Scheldt. 4×4in

1924 The Town Hall and Cathedral at Veere. Watercolour 22 × 16½in

spindly bulbous tower of the Radhuis. He met a Dutch artist who took him sailing on the Veersegat and through the Zaandkreek. The low horizons, the great cumulus-piled skies, the reedbeds and the wild fowl were to become a lasting influence on his work. When he himself bought a small sailing boat, it was on the very similar waters of the Thames Estuary, the Medway and the Swale that he sailed. This early introduction to sailing in estuary waters provided a further dimension to his work as a marine artist.

From Veere he returned to Flushing, crossed the Scheldt to Breskens by the ferry, took a bus to the nice old town of Sluis and from Sluis took a passage on a canal boat to Bruges. He was almost overwhelmed by the beauty of this old Flemish city. He was also quite overcome by the stench of the canals when he spent a day rowing through the mediaeval network of waterways in a hired boat. Before rejoining his ship, Rowland Hilder made one more diversion to Ghent to look at the Breughels in the Musée des Beaux Arts.

In the following year he signed on as a purser again and made two very rough trips up to Scotland and another which took him up the

1925 Down channel, the coast of Cornwall. Page from sketch-book drawn
on a coastal voyage to Manchester. Actual size

1924 Rough sea from the beach. Pencil drawing 8 × 13in

1926 Fishing boats at Rye. Pencil and wash drawing $7\frac{1}{2} \times 16$in

Ship Canal to Manchester. He followed this with a long voyage out of Scarborough with the fishing fleet and was sick the whole time! His visual notes made at sea are most evocative. Often they were no more than a slight little drawing with a faint wash of colour, only about three to four inches wide and one and a half to two inches high. Yet later they were to provide the bones for many paintings and illustrations.

Some pencil sketches made in the Irish Sea in a heavy gale off the Welsh coast are most telling. Whilst I was looking at these, Hilder said: 'It was blowing so hard that day that it was impossible to stand against the force of the wind.' He paused for a moment to look at one little drawing. 'I made these little notes jammed into a corner of the deck in the lee of a deckhouse.' The scene was already etched in his mind, but these slight sketches helped to reinforce his visual memory. The fact that quite a large coaster can be tossed about like a little dinghy is not something one would think of drawing unless one had seen it.

Notes like these showing how ships act under stress of wind and sea and endless studies of ships and boats at anchor and ashore were to provide the backbone to the marine illustrations he was soon to undertake. Hilder possesses a rare ability of not only being able to draw a ship or a boat so that it looks right at sea whether under way or at anchor, but he also conveys the texture of the steel plates of the hull and the feel of the flax or the canvas of the sails. From looking at the drawing he did in 1926 of a clinker-built fishing boat in Rye harbour, anyone who knows enough about boat

1925 Sketches of steamer in a gale in the Irish Sea off the Welsh coast. $6\frac{1}{2} \times 8$in

1923 Sea Reach off Southend. Page from sketch-book. $2 \times 4\frac{1}{2}$in actual size

1926 Watercolour drawing of a grain ship lying off Greenwich. $8 \times 10\frac{1}{2}$in

building could practically reconstruct the lines of this local fishing boat. The way she leans over to port and sits rather heavily on her flat bilge, the tautness of her starboard shrouds and the slackness of those on the port side could only be drawn by someone who has a real knowledge of boats and is also the possessor of a great natural talent in drawing. There can seldom have been an art student so well endowed with drawing ability as Rowland Hilder was. There certainly has not been in our lifetime a marine artist who could draw like him.

In 1924 to help support himself, Hilder was lucky enough to find a two-day-a-week job in the London studio of Henry Stone & Co., the Banbury printers. He aroused some envy in the studio when he was sent off to Liverpool to do a series of drawings of the interiors of a new 14,000-ton cargo liner, the *Ascania*. These quite elaborate architectural drawings were reproduced in a handsome brochure. Apart from that, little work of any interest came his way.

1936 Rowland Hilder tightening up a shroud aboard his yacht *Grateful*

1925 Charcoal drawing of the 14,000-ton Cunarder *Ascania*, drawn by Rowland Hilder whilst working for Stone & Co.

1926 Cable ship at Greenwich. Pencil drawing $17\frac{1}{2} \times 28$in

He was still attending Goldsmith's for three days a week. When he was only eighteen he exhibited at both the Royal Academy and the New English Art Club. The exhibit at the R.A. was a large drawing of a cable ship. It was bought by two Royal Academicians, William Orpen and Arnesby Brown, on behalf of the National Gallery of Australia in New South Wales. This drawing had been seen by two ladies, Miss Sharman and Miss Middleton, who ran an artists' agency which they called for obvious reasons 'Sharmid'. Whilst he was still at Stone's, Sharmid commissioned Hilder to do a book jacket for a publisher who happened to be one of Stone's customers. When Stone's discovered this, they sacked him on the spot. He had been there one year and all he had learned, so he said,'was how to spend eight hours a day doing two hours work'.

The pencil drawings of the cable ship and of the grain elevator with a sailing barge in the foreground are virtuoso performances. For some obscure reason the cable ship drawing has two dates on it: the title 'Cable ship, Greenwich' and 1926 and the artist's signature and 1927. The watercolour of the Thames at Rotherhithe is yet another example of Hilder's instinctive sense of perspective. The little tug in the background is sitting firmly in the water, which is in fact nothing but the white paper on which the drawing is done.

1927 Grain elevator in Surrey Docks with sailing barge in foreground.
Pencil drawing 19½ × 27in

1926 The Thames at Rotherhithe. Watercolour drawing 6 × 10in

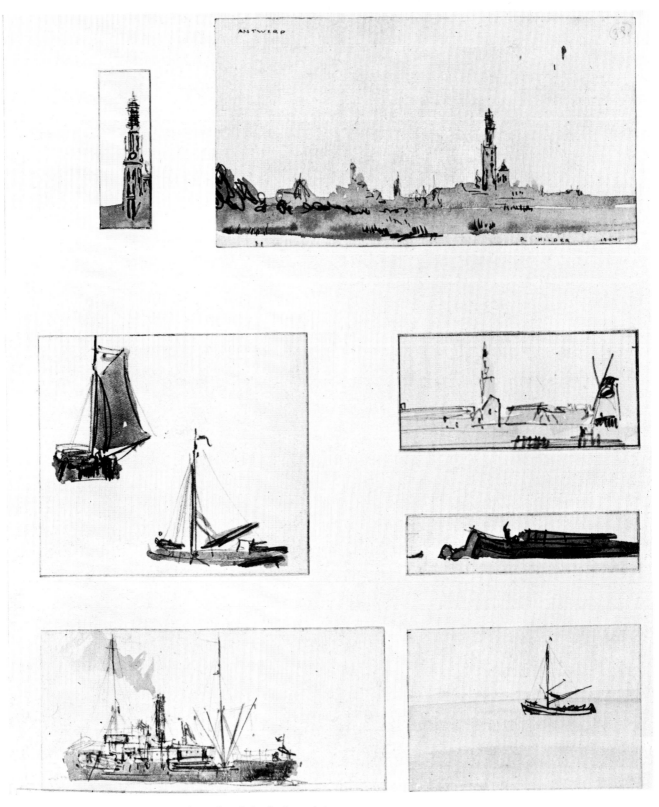

1924 Antwerp and shipping. Page from sketch-book. Actual size

These sketch-book drawings are exercises in observation. By such use of the sketch-book, the artist imprints these scenes on his mind. In contrast the next few pages show more elaborate studies made of ships at anchor.

1924 The skyline of Antwerp and shipping in the Scheldt. Page from
sketch-book. Actual size

1927 Watercolour study of the bow of a barge. $13\frac{1}{2} \times 17\frac{1}{2}$ in

1928 Sailing craft in the Medway with topsail schooner. $4\frac{1}{4} \times 7\frac{1}{4}$ in

1927 Watercolour study of the bow of a barge with rope fender. $13\frac{1}{2} \times 17\frac{1}{2}$in

1928 Pencil drawing of the barquentine *Ingomar*. 14 × 18in

1928 Pencil and wash drawing of the deck of a topsail schooner in the
Medway. $10\frac{1}{4} \times 9$in

The deck scene (above) is of the same topsail schooner shown in
the drawing on page 36. Though this deck scene is freely drawn,
there is enough information here to satisfy any ship model maker.
While Rowland Hilder was drawing the barquentine *Ingomar* (see
page 37) the crew offered to square off the yards and set the sails if
he would give them £5. He could not raise anything like that
amount, so he had to draw her as she was, with yards cockbilled.
The two watercolour studies of barges show an extraordinary
ability to reveal the texture of the old wooden planking, the
battered iron plates and the ravelled rope fender.

The studies overleaf show two views of the beach hut at Seasalter.
This hut was used by Rowland Hilder as a base for sailing
excursions to Whitstable or up the Swale to the creeks and saltings
of the Isle of Sheppey.

1932 Pencil drawing of steamer. 7 × 9in

1932 'Steamers on the Thames'. Pencil and watercolour drawing 7 × 9¾in

1927 Pencil drawing of Norman Hepple RA. Drawn in a warehouse at Rye on a bicycle tour of the south coast. $8\frac{1}{2} \times 7$in

Opposite: c.1930 Watercolour study of Richard Southern in the Hilders' beach hut at Seasalter, near Whitstable. $7\frac{3}{4} \times 10$in

c. 1930 Watercolour study of the Hilders' beach hut at Seasalter

1927 Pencil drawing of beach boats, drawn on the same tour. $6 \times 10\frac{1}{2}$in

1931 Railway wagons, dockside Whitstable. Conté pencil study

These studies were mostly drawn with either a conté or carbon pencil.

c.1936 Barley drying kiln with lock and weir, East Anglia. Watercolour and carbon pencil 7 × 9in

1930 Old Greenwich. Conté pencil study

1928 Pencil drawing of Faversham, Kent. Drawn whilst on a cruise from
Stoke in a converted lifeboat

1926 Endpaper design for *Moby Dick*

Part I

2. Book illustrations for sea stories.

After his abrupt departure from Stone's, Hilder continued to attend Goldsmith's, and hopefully to await further commissions. It was not long before Blackie's asked him, through his agent, to illustrate a boy's book, *The Riddle of the Air,* by Percy F. Westerman. These drawings, immature though they were, resulted in an introduction to Jonathan Cape. The year was 1925.

The firm of Cape was run by two widely differing men, Jonathan Cape and Wren Howard. Cape was a pioneering salesman with a great publishing flair. Howard, who looked like a retired Army Officer, was a quiet, thoughtful man with a real feeling for the design of books. Under Howard's guidance, Cape's books became renowned for the quality of their typography and their binding. Boys' books in the 1920s were unattractive things, usually printed on puffed-up stock with a surface like blotting paper. Wren Howard saw no reason why boys' books, and girls' for that matter, should not be as appealing as the books their parents read.

1926 Illustration for *Moby Dick*

One of the first juvenile books that Cape produced in this manner was an abridged edition of Herman Melville's *Moby Dick* and Rowland Hilder was asked to illustrate it. A tough proposition, for he had never been whaling and there was little available reference to do with nineteenth-century whalers.

There was, however, a silent film called *Down to the Sea in Ships* being shown at that time which had some quite good whaling shots. Rowland also found a copy of Frank Bullen's book *The Cruise of the Cachalot* which had been published in 1898. This had some tolerably good illustrations, particularly of whalers in close pursuit of the sperm whale. Apart from a couple of scientific books published in the first half of the nineteenth century, which gave him some background material, that was about all he could find. In spite of this the drawings in Hilder's *Moby Dick* are convincing. They are full of movement and in the case of the drawings of the whalers have an instinctive feeling for how a pulling boat acts in a seaway. This understanding of how boats and ships behave at sea and how the sea itself behaves was one of the factors that gave such distinction to Hilder's marine drawings. Having said this, the *Moby Dick* illustrations compared with his later work are somewhat uneven, and Sullivan's influence is still obvious. The most effective drawings in the book are the headpieces, the landscape shape suiting Hilder so much better than the upright plate formula. In these uprights, as if the constraint was too much, he has his figures partly stepping out of the frames. Hilder's *Moby Dick* drawings anticipated Rockwell Kent's edition for Random House by four or five years. Kent must have seen the Hilder version because there are one or two marked similarities, but as Hilder said 'My goodness, how he improved on them!'

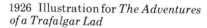

1926 Illustration for *The Adventures of a Trafalgar Lad*

1927 Double spread for *A Sailor of Napoleon*

Moby Dick was followed by four more boys' books for Cape, all written by John Lesterman. These were most attractive octavo books, bound in smooth dark blue cloth, blocked in gold with a coloured frontispiece, a fair scattering of line drawings through the text and in most cases with illustrated endpapers.

Already in the first of these, *The Adventures of a Trafalgar Lad*, the drawings have become much more assured than those in *Moby Dick*. He was making effective use of solid blacks, silhouettes and counterchange, though the figure drawings are still less appealing than the seascapes. In *A Sailor of Napoleon* (1927), the second of this series, Rowland Hilder collaborated with Richard Southern, his close friend and former fellow student at Goldsmith's. Southern, who later made his name in the theatre, already had a

1928 Illustrations for *A Pair of Rovers*

wide knowledge of costume. He provided this background material and Hilder did most of the drawings. This was followed by *A Pair of Rovers* in 1928. The paper used in these books, though not of the puffed-up sort, did not take fine line too well, so Hilder started using a brush rather than a pen, thus breaking with a long tradition of pen work. This tradition was established with the

1929 Illustrations for *The Second Mate of the Myradale*

introduction of the process line block, first by Edwin A. Abbey and Hugh Thomson, and later carried on by Howard Pyle, Edmund J. Sullivan and many others.

Rowland Hilder worked on the last of the series of the Lesterman books at High Halstow. It was called *The Second Mate of the Myradale* and was published by Cape in 1929. This was not only the best produced of the four books, but it had the best illustrations. Hilder's personal style of pen drawing was crystallizing and he was shedding the Sullivan influence.

1929 Two-colour drawing for endpapers for *Treasure Island*

All this time Rowland Hilder was working at home, paying his
parents rent for the room they had made over to him for a studio.
After a while this arrangement became rather confining and he
started to look around for a place of his own. One weekend when he
was staying with the Screetons at Allhallows, Bill Screeton
mentioned that a former pub called the Old Britannia at High
Halstow, about five miles from Allhallows, was to let. Rowland and
Norman Hepple, another, though younger, ex-student from
Goldsmith's, bicycled over to see it. They liked it, decided they
might share it, and took it for a year.

1928 Pencil study of Jim Hawkins for *Treasure Island*

1928 Pencil study for slipcase illustration for *Treasure Island*

1929 Illustration for the slipcase of *Treasure Island*

1928 Pencil study of trees in Greenwich park for illustration in *Treasure Island*

These Cape books that Rowland Hilder illustrated were a breakthrough in book illustration. Hilder, always a lateral thinker, found the upright single page format for illustrations too confining for a subject as expansive as the sea, so he introduced the double spread, even though each half of the illustration was enclosed in a frame of heavy black lines. Rowland Hilder's approach to illustration was that of the landscape painter. Such figures as there were, were seen in a setting. He brought the background into the picture. As the books progressed the figure drawings, where figures mattered, became much more assured and his use of unusual viewpoints, one might almost say in cinematic terms camera angles, gave a welcome freshness to the illustrations.

On the evidence of the Cape books, the Oxford University Press asked Rowland Hilder to illustrate the two Robert Louis Stevenson classics *Treasure Island* and *Kidnapped*, but being a conservatively minded house, they would have nothing to do with Hilder's double spreads. They demanded the conventional 'gift book' format established in the early years of the century by Rackham, Dulac, Kay Nielsen and Heath Robinson with a set of four-colour half-tone plates, twelve of them in all, mounted in the book with just a few supporting black and white drawings. The

1929 Illustration for Captain Silver from *Treasure Island*

1932 Illustration for *True Tales of the Sea*

only thing he felt he could do with these vertical plates was to make them into figure studies. Hilder, now a competent figure draughtsman, accepted the challenge. His preliminary drawings from models for the *Treasure Island* illustrations were almost Pre-Raphaelite, if not Düreresque, in his preoccupation with the folds of the clothing revealing the underlying human form. The book was published in 1929. It was handsomely bound and boxed and printed at the Oxford University Press. The colour plates were effective but the nicest illustrations were the black and white drawings for the various half-titles, drawings of Billy Bones, of Bristol Docks and of Captain Silver, and the splendid endpapers across which the schooner *Hispaniola* went sailing full and by.

There is only one comparable edition of *Treasure Island* and that is the one illustrated by the American N. C. Wyeth in 1912. Wyeth's are firm, robust drawings and I think any boy would have been delighted to have had either the Wyeth or the Hilder version of Stevenson's marvellous story.

Kidnapped which came out in the following year, was a competent professional job, but the subject, the background of the Western Isles, was one for a painter. At that stage in his career Rowland Hilder was still primarily a draughtsman.

1930 Illustration to *Kidnapped*

There is a wry footnote to the *Treasure Island* story. The Oxford University Press, who owned the originals, lent them to the Victoria and Albert Museum for some book illustration exhibition from which apparently they were stolen. In the 1970s Oxford once again re-issued Hilder's *Treasure Island*.

1931 Illustration for *The Midnight Folk* 'Captain Harker bound and gagged'

In 1932 Hilder illustrated one more sea book, again for Oxford. This was C. Fox Smith's *True Tales of the Sea*. For these illustrations he evolved a more formal engraved style of line work with a second printing in khaki yellow. The book, however, was ruined by being printed on puffed-up stock which blurred the pen lines. There was, however, an attractive coloured frontispiece of a clipper with furled sails lying alongside the old Pagoda anchorage on the river Min in Foochow. This was a picture that evoked thoughts of a time when the tea trade appeared to be nothing but a romantic struggle between flying clippers racing from China to London river. This frontispiece was actually drawn in pastel and chalk many times larger than the printed size. It was the fore-runner of many such romantic paintings that he was to do in years to come. In contrast to the rather formalised two-colour engraving-style illustrations which were double spreads, the black and white drawings in the text were much freer than any he had done before.

The romantic urge that had sent the young Rowland Hilder bicycling miles through the docks to see the grain ships and the timber barques was evident in all this illustration work. Ultimately it was to be one of the conditioning factors in his development as a painter.

As a result of *Treasure Island*, John Masefield personally commissioned Rowland Hilder to illustrate *The Midnight Folk*. Hilder said that Masefield was a delight to work with. He stayed with the Poet Laureate at both Boar's Hill and later at Cirencester. *The Midnight Folk* should have been Hilder's best illustrated book, but it turned out, so he said, to be a sad disappointment. He had planned the illustrations to be colour

1931 Illustration for *The Midnight Folk* 'They were playing chess'

double spreads printed by offset, but in the end Heinemann, the publisher, would have none of it. The book was being rushed out for the Christmas market, so the double spreads, by means of paste and scissors and some re-working, had to be converted into single page plates to be printed by four-colour letterpress. The woodenness of some of the figures is in part due to this cut-out process. Even so, one or two of the plates, such as the one of 'Parties of Knights returning from quests', gives some idea of how rich and colourful these pictures might have been. The black and white drawings are unevenly scattered through the book. The drawings of Kay's toys were actually done from the toys that had belonged to Masefield's children. There are not many sea subjects, but there is a spirited double spread of a French squadron in pursuit of an English ship and the drawing of Captain Harker, bound and gagged by a mutinous crew, is quietly dramatic and beautifully drawn. There is also an interesting study of chessmen playing chess by themselves. It shows what an instinctive grasp of perspective Hilder has always had.

When we were discussing this book, Rowland said: 'I still feel badly about *The Midnight Folk*. I feel I let John Masefield down. He had such faith in me. He was so charming, so very kind. He was in fact the soul of generosity.'

Forty years after the first publication of *The Midnight Folk* Heinemann had enough faith in this illustrated edition to re-issue it but this time for reasons of cost without the colour illustrations.

3. *Precious Bane* and the English landscape in winter

As a result of the success of the illustrations for the Lesterman sea
stories, Wren Howard at Cape asked Rowland Hilder if he would
be willing to switch his attention from seascape to landscape. The
project Cape had in mind was a series of illustrated editions of
Mary Webb's books. The countryside was that of south
Shropshire, with the one exception of her most famous work,
Precious Bane, which was set in the Ellesmere district of north
Shropshire. This is the country of the Severn lowlands and solitary
upland ridges.

In the 1920s a number of nostalgic books about the English
countryside appeared. These were the successors to Thomas
Hardy's Wessex novels. Mary Webb's fame was consolidated when
Stanley Baldwin, the Conservative Prime Minister, expressed his
appreciation for her work when addressing a dinner in support of
the Royal Literary Fund on 26 April 1928. He followed this up by
writing a lengthy foreword to the new illustrated edition of
Precious Bane. Town dwellers, at least in those days, felt that they
still had roots in the country.

Publishers, when they finally make up their wandering minds,
always want a book in a hurry. Cape was no exception, and though
it was winter time, Wren Howard arranged for Rowland Hilder to
stay in Mary Webb's cottage at Lyth Hill to get a feeling of the
place. Rowland and Edith, his wife-to-be, and his mother who acted
both as chaperone and housekeeper to them, moved down to Lyth
Hill at the beginning of November and stayed there for six weeks.
Rowland recalls that it was bitterly cold and staying in Mary
Webb's cottage was a somewhat spooky experience. It seemed to be
haunted not only by the ghost of that poor sick lady (who had
suffered for many years from Graves's disease), but also was filled
with all the objects she had described in her books, including a
particular clock with pictures on its face. Over the mantelpiece
there were a pair of oars, for Mr Webb had rowed for his college at
Cambridge.

In spite of the cold, Hilder was struck by the sheer stark beauty of
the frost-rimmed furrows and the tall leafless elms. This was the
moment of truth. Here was a theme so powerful, so strong and with
so great a pictorial effect that it had an overwhelming effect on
him, yet no English artist had touched it, except perhaps Turner.

Rowland Hilder, used as he was to sailing on the Thames in winter
time, was well fitted for this wintry sketching. He set out day after
day to draw the countryside and the barns, the churches with their
lych gates, and the farm wagons. He was particularly good at
drawing wagon wheels, which was something he had learnt from
studying the drawings of Muirhead Bone. These drawings were to

1928 The wheelwright's shop at High Halstow. Pencil study for *Precious Bane* $10 \times 8\frac{1}{4}$ in

1929 'Ploughing'. Double-spread illustration for *Precious Bane*

1929 'Winter Trees' illustration for *Precious Bane*

provide the background to the story. The landscape was to become an integral part of the illustrations.

He and Edith met various people who had known Mary Webb, from the time when she and her husband were living at Pontisbury (they moved later to Lyth Hill), when Mary Webb was working as a market gardener and sold fruit and vegetables at her own stall in Shrewsbury market, until her last years, when, poor creature, she was very ill and had become quite disorientated in her mind. An old man told the Hilders how he had seen Mary Webb, not long before she died, rush down a hill into a field of ripening corn and throw herself into it, trying to embrace the whole field.

Hilder responded to this strange and powerful tale – the story of a girl with a hare-shotten lip and her money-hungry brother. But even more he responded to the cold, wintry beauty of the Shropshire countryside.

Rowland Hilder comes of Kentish stock. There is a hamlet in Kent called Hilders and there used to be a farm in East Sussex that since Doomsday had been known as Hilder's farm. The Hilders were not only yeoman farmers; every so often they produced an artist. Brett

1929 Rough sketch for 'Mug of Cider' illustration,
Precious Bane

1929 Study for 'Mug of Cider' illustration,
Precious Bane

1929 Rough sketch for 'I saw the wagon from Plash',
Precious Bane

1928 Study for 'I saw the wagon from Plash',
Precious Bane

1929 The final drawing for 'Mug of Cider',
Precious Bane

1929 The final drawing for 'I saw the wagon from Plash',
Precious Bane

1929 The 'censored' drawing for *Precious Bane*

Hilder, the Australian painter, in his book *The Heritage of J. J. Hilder*, traces three branches of Hilders, who between them had produced eleven or twelve artists of varying talents. A feeling for the countryside was in Rowland's blood, but this was the first time that anything had really aroused such feelings.

Precious Bane could not be illustrated entirely as if Shropshire was a country to be seen only in winter, so Hilder clothed the trees and allowed the lilies to bloom on Sarn Mere; the figure drawings he completed after he had returned to his Blackheath studio. They ranged from quite free drawings to careful studies, including one drawing of the naked Pru Sarn entitled *The raising of Venus*. This drawing Cape rejected on the grounds that it might shock their readers.

When the illustrations for the book were completed, there were four colour plates as well as many black and white drawings. The strength of the book lay in the latter, which vary from heavily

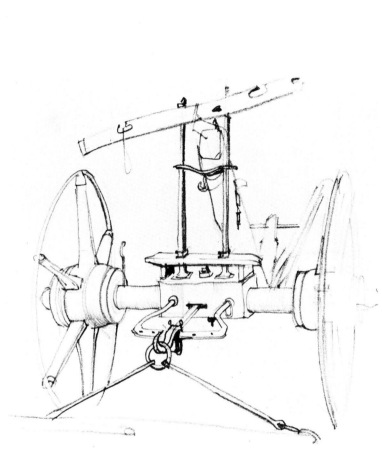

c.1928 Pencil study of farm machinery

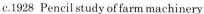

1928 Wagon wheels. Pencil study $10 \times 5\frac{1}{2}$in

framed, woodcut-like brush drawings to freely vignetted line drawings. He relied heavily on chiaroscuro, a useful device for concealing the heroine's hare-lip. It was, however, a technique that was easy to plagiarize, as the illustrations to the other titles in the series show only too clearly.

There is one particular illustration, a double spread of a wide winter landscape drawn from the side of a hill, which is of some significance. Far below can be seen the hardly identifiable figure of Gideon Sarn at his eternal ploughing. This and one vignetted drawing of a wintry rookery are the forerunners of a thousand leafless trees that Rowland Hilder was to draw in the years ahead.

It was *Precious Bane* that diverted Rowland Hilder from a career of marine illustration into painting the English landscape and particularly the English landscape in winter time. The Jonathan Cape directors unknowingly had launched him on a new career.

1929 Illustration for *Then and Now*, published by Shell Mex Ltd

The first step into this landscape business occured when Fred Beddington, who had studied at the Slade and was later to work for Wildenstein's, the Bond Street Art dealers, on the strength of the *Precious Bane* drawings, recommended Hilder to the notice of his brother Jack.

Jack Beddington was a Shell Oil man who at that time had recently returned from China and had been put in charge of the firm's publicity. At that stage, although he had been at Balliol and was a man of some culture, he knew little about the English art scene, so he naturally turned to his artistic younger brother for advice. In discussing this, Fred Beddington said quite recently, 'I may have known more than Jack did about the art scene, but, my goodness, he soon outstripped me. He had an absolute flair for picking winners.'

The result was a Shell 'stable' of artists as diverse as Paul Nash, Graham Sutherland, L. S. Lowry, John Armstrong and E. McKnight Kauffer, who had also been introduced by Fred Beddington to his brother. These artists were intended to be used for poster work. For press work the list was headed by Rex Whistler, Nicolas Bentley, Rowland Hilder and later by Edward Bawden. Rowland Hilder illustrated advertising booklets, one on the history of the road and another about the pollution of rivers. His skill as an architectural draughtsman was brought into play when he did a big drawing of the completed Grosvenor House Hotel in Park Lane (whilst it was only half built). This was to advertise Shell's entry into the central heating market.

Again on the success of the *Precious Bane* drawings, Hilder's agent sold some more of his winter landscape drawings to Pratt Oil which did not please Shell. The Pratt drawings had such a response that Pratt had an edition specially printed on hand-made paper. I remember Freddy Beddington showing me these special reproductions before I had even become an art student. I wrote to Pratt for a set. In fact the impression on newsprint was far better than those especially printed on rather soft rag paper. Their advertisements were aimed at persuading motorists to use their motor cars in winter, by extolling the beauty of the English landscape during those months.

It seems curious, forty years on, to think the motorist needed any persuasion to use his motor car at any time. In fact in the 1930s it was common practice to lay up your car in the winter months. The press comments that these Rowland Hilder advertisements evoked are revealing. *World's Press News* said, 'Selling the winter countryside in this way is a sure way of selling more petrol . . . there

1929 Drawing of the new Grosvenor House
Hotel, before it was built

1932 Illustrations for *In Defence of British
Rivers*, published by Shell Mex and BP Ltd

1933 Pen drawing for press advertisement for
Pratt Oil Ltd

are still thousands of owner-drivers in this country who are
susceptible to these suggestions conveyed in Rowland Hilder's
finely realistic drawings.' (This last remark was in reference to a
drawing in which an out-of-scale cart-horse had been put into
Hilder's drawing by a studio hack!). *Autocar's* words were 'The
beautiful drawings by Rowland Hilder will really work the oracle
and send people out into the fresh air, thus serving the trade in this
country.' *Advertiser's Weekly* comments were: 'Rowland Hilder
has caught the spirit of the winter landscape with a skill which is
magical...'

It was these advertisements, first appearing only in the *Sunday
Times* and *The Observer* but later displayed in the popular
national dailies, that made Rowland Hilder's name so widely
known.

1933 Pen drawing for press advertisement for
Pratt Oil Ltd

Meanwhile Cape had sold the rights of some of the *Precious Bane*
drawings to the Medici Gallery, who added their own colour to the
designs and marketed them as Christmas cards, and also as
stick-on labels. Hilder never got a penny out of this, but as
Laurence Irving wrote at the time: 'You have swept the
overmantels of Britain.' Hilder had no rights in these drawings,
but Medici had contravened a little-known law, based on the
precedent of the 'Garth Jones' case which forbade alteration to a
work of art without the artist's permission. As a recompense,
Medici offered Hilder a contract to do a number of Christmas card
designs for them at five guineas each. They made it clear to him
that three guineas was their normal fee.

The spread of Hilder's Christmas cards for the first year or so
through Medici and then through the Ward Gallery made Rowland

1936 Sunset on a river. Reproduced by the
Ward Gallery as a Christmas card

c.1930 Illustration from *Precious Bane*, issued
by the Medici Society as a Christmas card and
stick-on label

Hilder's name and his winter landscapes familiar to an even wider
market. The Medici cards were well produced, sometimes
combining in a pleasant way a black line with stencilled
watercolour washes. The Ward Gallery cards were more
economically printed, often in black or a single colour or in
hand-separated colours with the use of tints. These coloured cards
were printed by the Edinburgh firm of McLagan and Cumming;
where full colour was needed, they used the by then out-dated
three-colour process, printing from the three primary colours and
leaving out the black. It was not, however, until some years later
when Hilder, with the help of his father, took over the publication
of his Christmas cards that the drawings received the treatment
they deserved.

As a result of the success of the Shell and Pratt advertisements,
and of the Medici Gallery marketing his *Precious Bane* drawings,
Rowland Hilder, for better or worse, became firmly established in
the world of commercial illustration. The pattern of his
professional life was set for the next twenty years.

Part 2

1 A series of paradoxes

The first of these paradoxes was that Hilder was a precociously brilliant draughtsman whose development as a serious painter did not match this precocity. Painting after all is much more than a matter of sleight of hand. It is an endlessly developing mental process, a search for a motive and for a satisfactory means of expressing it.

The second was that what Hilder wanted to do – to paint landscapes and seascapes in a tradition that had started with Ruisdael and Hobbema and reached fruition with Turner – was being dismissed by the critics and the supporters of the modern movement as being completely irrelevant to the times. All the traditional skills and attitudes that Rowland Hilder had been taught were suddenly discredited.

Lastly, the sudden burst of success he had had as a popular artist, with his winter landscape drawings for advertisements and Christmas cards, led him into an apparently endless vista of commercial work. His great skill as a draughtsman was his undoing and was, of course, one of the reasons for his success. That and the fact that his Pratt oil drawings were something quite new. Nothing like them had ever been used in advertising before. The result of this was that he was soon inundated with work from commercial houses and advertising studios.

'One of the troubles, the difficulties of all this, was that I don't think I was any good as a commercial artist', Hilder remarked recently. The techniques of drawing that he had learned from following Dürer and Rembrandt were far too cumbersome for this ephemeral, fly-by-night advertising stuff. Nevertheless work poured in from the railway companies and the airlines, the Post Office and London Transport and above all from the advertising agencies.

Over and above this was a continuing contract with the Ward Gallery for twenty-eight Christmas cards each year. At the same time he was teaching at Goldsmith's, having taken over Sullivan's job; he was lecturing to the Art Workers' Guild and to students from the Slade, the Royal College and the Central School. He was also helping Milner Gray and others to establish the Society of Industrial Artists. Meanwhile he was still drawing and painting both the sea and the land, much of this work being diverted into reproduction and no doubt suffering from the exigencies of process and the need for overstatement to get satisfactory results.

Hilder was also one of the last recording news illustrators. For the Jubilee Review in 1935 he was sent by *The Sphere* to draw the fleet which was lined up at Spithead. The naval craft provided for him

1928 Smith's Farm, High Halstow. Carbon pencil and watercolour
drawing $6\frac{1}{2} \times 12$in

1935 Watercolour drawing of Stoke Halt. This drawing was done whilst
on a cruise from Whitstable to the Blackwater $5\frac{1}{2} \times 11\frac{1}{2}$in

1932 Watercolour and conté pencil drawing of the Thames at Greenwich.
$4\frac{3}{4} \times 6\frac{3}{4}$ in

for some reason went the wrong way so he had to land and find a
motor-boat, which finally reached the fleet as it was getting dark
and just as one of the biggest firework displays that has ever been
held was about to start. So he drew that, much to the annoyance of
The Sphere. However, they featured it as a double spread and it
was widely applauded. His excursion to Westminster Abbey to
draw Princess Marina's wedding was less successful. He had set up
his easel in a special place allotted to him opposite the Abbey,
when the barricades behind him broke. The crowd surged forward
and knocked him and his easel flying and then trampled all over
him. So he never saw that either, but even so he turned in a
drawing which must have depended mainly on his imagination.

There were, of course, economic reasons for all this. His fee for
illustrating *Treasure Island,* which took six months' hard work,
was £120. He could not support a wife on that kind of money.
Hence the sallies into commercial work. He was still trying to
paint, but was not selling many pictures. It is not easy to be a
Sunday painter if you are a week-day commercial artist. The odds
are you may become a Sunday commercial artist as well. Most
artists suffer from some conflict between their spiritual hopes and
the pragmatic expedients to which they are compelled to resort in
order to live.

By the mid-1930s, Rowland Hilder was being accepted by a very
wide public. In England he was *the* popular artist of the time yet it
was the last thing he wanted. He felt, quite rightly, that he did not
fit in anywhere. He certainly did not fit in with the modern

1962 'The Garden of England'. Watercolour and ink drawing 20 × 30in

movement, nor did he fit in with the Royal Academy either, yet as a draughtsman, if not as a painter, at that time, he was more academic than any of them. It was not surprising that he developed an obsessive neurosis as an outcome of these tensions. He was constantly feeling sick. It was some years before he was able to put all this behind him. Neurotic or not, he still had to work.

In 1935 his first oil painting to receive any notice was hung in the Royal Academy. It was a scene, painted on a June morning, of a winding road leading down to a group of tall elms and some hayricks, flanked by ploughed fields and growing crops. This road seems to lead one into a never-never land of rural contentment. The few figures in the middle distance are so unimportant, they can be disregarded.

This, looking back, was an important landmark. It was his first serious attempt to become a painter. In the same year he was elected to the Royal Institute of Watercolour Painters and soon after that he had his first one-man show at Brighton, which resulted in a long article in *The Studio*.

A watercolour drawing, also exhibited at that time at the Royal Academy, was of a winter scene of ploughed fields and leafless elm trees, with a range of hills in the blue distance. This was reproduced by Medici and was published as a postcard. It was the first of many such wintry scenes.

Anthony Quinton, in his BBC programme *Letter from London,* BBC World Service 25–26 October 1975, described most aptly what made these winter landscapes so popular. 'They are very much my own idea of what a Christmas card emanating from an English address should be. I send them with resolution and receive them with delight.

'The usual scene is a large ploughed field late in autumn or early in winter, with nothing yet growing visibly on it. The field is of a humped, undulating shape, the kind of thing commonly found in Sussex and Hampshire. There is a thatched barn, of slightly desolate, but nevertheless solid, and well-constructed appearance, near some corner of the field, and by it a group of elms.

'This is my ideal landscape, without people but with clear signs of elemental life, absolutely free from any sign of the technical progress of the age...'

Rowland Hilder, with these reproductions of his wintry Kentish scenes, created a vision so appealing that it became part of everybody's idea of what the English landscape looked like in

1935 'Threshing'. Pen and watercolour drawing 8½ × 12in

winter time. J. B. J. Peel, writing in an article called 'Ports of Call', which was published in the *Daily Telegraph* Supplement in December 1970, summed it up when he said, 'This is border country where Kent meets Sussex, the marshes are thick with sheep, the Downs of the latter are alight with red-tiled barns and a *Rowland Hilderscape* of wintry trees.' His name had become part of the national vocabulary.

As the 1930s came to their half-way mark, Hilder's commercial work continued, but some jobs were less odious than others. Amongst these was a set of very handsome jackets for the first editions of C. S. Forester's 'Hornblower' books. He obviously enjoyed doing these. It must have seemed like a welcome return to earlier days when he had been working for Cape. At the same time he became great friends with Forester.

Whether or not it was because of doing these seafaring jackets, his Christmas cards suddenly assumed a more maritime aspect. The subjects were of old sailing ships, battered sailing smacks or even beach boats, as often as not resting alongside remote quays or anchored in still waters, or pulled up above the tide line. The mood of all these – and this feeling of mood is what his art is all about – is one of tranquillity.

1935 'The farm road'. Oil on canvas 20 × 24in. Reproduced by the Medici
Society

1936 English Landscape. Watercolour painting 33 × 48½in. Reproduced by
the Ward Gallery as a Christmas card

1937 Calendar design for McLagan and Cumming

Rowland Hilder's fame may at the moment rest on his paintings of a wintry Kentish landscape, yet his marine work is even more personal. Much of it is romantic stuff, evoking memories of the Pagoda anchorage and flying clippers and of Trafalgar and the 'old wooden walls', to a degree seen through other eyes, through those of Dutch painters, such as Jan van de Cappelle and Turner. Yet these pictures are raised from what might seem to be a second-hand vision by his drawing ability and sheer knowledge of ships and the sea.

One can forgive all the romantic excesses in Hilder's work because of the quality of the drawing in such pictures as that of his little sailing punt on page 77. (I learned to sail in this little boat later.)

Drawings like this and the one of the sluice gate on page 78, with its close-up view of a muddy little ditch surmounted by tufts of marram grass, bending before the East Anglian wind that never seems to stop blowing over the saltings, or the detail of the capstan in the drawing on page 79 are what lift his romantic drawings out of mere sentimental recall, into an area that might be called 'romantic realism'. This may seem a contradiction in terms, yet in the picture above, though a romantic subject with the barquentine inevitably evoking memories of a golden past, the two open boats in the foreground are firmly drawn and beautifully realised. They could be any open boats chocked up on any quayside or foreshore today. This is a drawing based on observation.

1926 The frontispiece of *A Sailor of Napoleon*. Watercolour and gouache

1935 'Low tide'. Christmas Card design for the Ward Gallery

The fact that his ships and boats rest on the mud at low water, or are pulled clear of the sea on shingle beaches, or are lying securely anchored in safe harbours reflects the attitude of anyone who has sailed the seas in small yachts or deep-sea traders. The moment of contentment comes when they are safely in port and all that endless turmoil has been left behind. Not for such mariners are the pictures of dis-masted clippers or small coasters running on to the rocks. That is the stuff for romantic landsmen. It is not inconceivable that the sailors would like Rowland Hilder's pictures of rural England even more than they like his paintings of safely docked vessels.

1932 Watercolour drawing of 'the Punt'. From this little boat Rowland Hilder made many of his marine drawings. $6 \times 8\frac{3}{4}$in

Hilder has continued to sail. He bought his first boat, a flat-bottomed lug-rigged Medway punt, in 1928. From this little boat he did many drawings. He sailed her from the Greenwich Yacht Club in Bugsby's Reach up to Tower Bridge and down to the Medway, through the Swale to Seasalter near Whitstable. On one rather more venturesome occasion he sailed across the estuary to the river Blackwater and got caught out in a bit of a blow. Finally he grounded on the Buxey Sands, bailed out the boat, put on dry trousers, made himself a cup of tea, then, with a fair tide under him, sailed into Brightlingsea to find that gale cones had been hoisted.

1935 Sluice gate on the Blackwater. Watercolour and carbon pencil
drawing 9 × 12in

Detail of *Int* Rye Harbour.

1927 The Capstan, a drawing made on the deck of a sailing coaster in Rye Harbour. $9 \times 7\frac{1}{4}$in

This periodic escape to the sea, or to the little beach hut they had at Seasalter, was a marvellous relaxation. For artists and designers who virtually live their work, a small boat is one way of clearing their minds of all their shore-based worries. Once you are in a boat there is another complete set of worries to obliterate the customary ones. These are worries about whether you are going to miss the tide, or going to be wrecked or even drowned, or, and this is a more usual one, what you are going to have for supper. It helped to keep Rowland Hilder sane.

1934 Woods and Forests. Advertisement drawing for London Transport

1934 Kentish Hopfields. Advertisement
drawing for London Transport

Part 2

2. The world of the commercial illustrator

In November 1935 the Hilders moved from their flat in Lee Park to the other side of Blackheath. After a long period of hunting for flats, the house agent suggested they should go and look at a large house in Kidbrooke Grove which had been empty for some years.

Numbers 5 and 7 Kidbrooke Grove make up a pair of tall gaunt four-storey grey brick semi-detached Victorian houses, set back from the road with a sweep of gravel drive in front of them and pretty walled gardens at the back. At a first glance Number 5 (the one for sale) must have seemed somewhat intimidating. It had large high rooms with great marble mantelpieces and ornate corniced ceilings. Acres of material would be needed to curtain the windows. The prevailing colour scheme was drab and dark, yet they began to see the possibilities of the Victorian drawing-rooms and their potential for studios. What was more, there was certainly a lot of house for the money. After a night of heart searching, they took it. Bit by bit they re-decorated it and after a while Rowland's parents and his sister moved into the first floor and they let off the two attics to two ex-Goldsmith's students. One of these was a boy called Cedric Rogers, who spent most of his waking hours playing the clarinet. He was the son of Stanley Rogers, artist and marine historian and a friend of the Hilders. I was the other lodger.

By the time I had arrived, the transformation of the house was well advanced. In due course, the Hilders bought it from their landlord and later on bought No. 7 as well. Ultimately these houses were to become a veritable power house of creative activity.

In the following April, their son Anthony was born. It was a happy, if hectic, household, with Rowland working at his drawing-board all hours of the day and night. I think it must have been the result of seeing Rowland Hilder being subjected to the pressures of all the false urgencies of advertising that I began to have doubts about my capabilities of earning my living as an illustrator. Not the least of Rowland's problems were his agents, first Don Chandler and later Tommy Thompson, who so forced up the price of his work that the advertising agencies started doing imitation Hilders themselves. Only when the jobs proved too difficult for the agency artists were they passed on to Hilder, who not only got these daunting jobs but had to complete them by impossible deadlines, to make up for all the time the agency had wasted.

In the two years of 1935 and 1936, the amount of work Hilder got through was prodigious and this on top of moving house and having a son born. As well as the fifty-six Christmas cards for the Ward Gallery, he was doing publicity pen drawings for the London and North Eastern Railway, conté and wash drawings of giant aeroplanes for Imperial Airways, line drawings for the Post Office, book jackets for various publishers, including those for Forester's 'Hornblower' books; drawings for *Good Housekeeping*, for Rowntrees and for *The Sphere* (according to his diary for 1935 one of these was rejected). He was working for Milner Gray's Industrial Design Partnership, he illustrated a sea story for Müller called *Fire Down Below* with pleasantly free pen drawings and he drew a Suffolk barn for *Nash's magazine*. He was also exhibiting paintings at Brighton (his first one-man show), at the Royal Academy, at the R.I. and at the Society of Marine Artists. There was another article about his work in *The Studio* and he was still teaching two days a week at Goldsmith's; another tutor there, a Royal Academician called James 'Cow' Bateman (so-called because of a painting exhibited at Burlington House entitled *Cows in Rickyard* which had achieved some notice), told Hilder what a rotten painter he was! It is not surprising that he so often felt sick.

Amongst his friends at that time, Hilder was seeing a lot of Douglas Percy Bliss, who afterwards became Principal of the Glasgow School of Art, C. S. Forester, whom he had first met at Stanley Rogers's house, Laurence Irving, another marine artist, as well as a stage designer, who was the grandson of the actor Sir Henry Irving. Laurence Irving lived in a beautifully converted windmill above Whitstable, and in the following year took Hilder sailing down Channel to Cornwall. Another, and for a while close friend, was H. A. Manhood, the author of the Hardyesque novel *Gay Agony*. There were also numerous Goldsmith's contemporaries, such as C. Walter Hodges, John Pimlott, Milner Gray and Stanley Froud with whom Rowland often sailed in company. There was nearly always someone or other calling in at Kidbrooke Grove, but Rowland was usually glued to his desk, seemingly oblivious to the noise round him. Edith was always in the background brewing cups of tea or helping in a hundred different ways.

Among the press drawings that Rowland Hilder drew in the following year was a series for Hartley's jam. There seems to have been a coarsening of technique, probably due to the severe reduction they had to withstand. The by now inevitable late afternoon scene, with very black shadows, was becoming a bit of a cliché. The pressures were beginning to tell and his work was suffering. His railway publicity drawings were also becoming a bit mannered. There is a hint of the influence of Rockwell Kent in the evenly ruled skies, but these are on the whole more sensitive than some of his other press drawings.

The Christmas cards designed at this time vary in quality: they mostly have simple, sometimes purposely over-stated colour schemes. Constantly working for reproduction in those days could

1938 Book jacket for *The Captain from Connecticut*. Watercolour drawing

1932 Watercolour and conté pencil drawing of the Thames at Greenwich.
$4\frac{3}{4} \times 6\frac{3}{4}$ in

bedevil an artist's work. Today with the perfection of the
four-colour process, for either letterpress or offset printing, the
situation is very different, but even here with reduction in size may
come the falsifying of tones. Some of the Ward Gallery cards had
quite jarring notes of colour, particularly a viridian green that
used to appear in the marine pictures.

In 1938 Hilder was approached by John Stirling who had had an
idea for an illustrated Bible. Stirling had spent some years trying
to get this book launched without any success. After some
discussion Rowland prepared various layouts showing the form
the Bible might take and also how it could be illustrated by

1937 'In the Days of Sail'. Three-colour pen drawing, reproduced as a
Christmas card by the Ward Gallery

contemporary scenes of industrial and rural life. On the strength
of these layouts, the Oxford University Press accepted the project.
Hilder had rather hoped that his part in the job would end there,
but Stirling persuaded him to set a style for the illustrations by
drawing just a few of them and then to find a team of like-minded
artists to do the rest. In fact, but most reluctantly, Rowland Hilder
did the bulk of these black and white drawings with some
contributions from, amongst others, John Pimlott, C. Walter
Hodges and Frances Hilder (Rowland's younger sister). It took
three years to complete. Inevitably *The Bible for Today* is an
uneven production. Hilder himself does not like it, but it sold in
thousands.

1939 Poster for the National Savings Group. 'Convoy your Country to Victory'

By 1939, it had become quite clear to Rowland Hilder that he was not getting an adequate return for all the work he was doing for the Christmas card market and he was becoming tired of drawing for advertising agencies. He had a vision of setting himself up as his own printer-publisher. Before he could take any positive action in this, the war started and the advertising world virtually collapsed.

Laurence Irving, who was with the R.A.F., recommended Hilder for the post of their official war artist. This was widely approved, but at the last moment was vetoed by the committee concerned. Keith Henderson, a somewhat unlikely substitute, was appointed. However, Hilder was soon employed in working on the project *Recording Britain,* doing drawings of Sussex for the Pilgrim Trust. He was also doing publicity work for the R.A.F.

In the autumn of 1939, the Hilders temporarily moved from Blackheath to a house in Caterham, which area they thought might be safer. He was working hard to complete the drawings for *The Bible for Today,* as well as doing work for the R.A.F. I remember telephoning him some time in April 1940 to tell him that he had been accepted as an Army Camouflage Officer.

'Well, I can't come today,' he replied. 'I am in the middle of bombing the Rhine, at least I am in the middle of drawing a Blenheim doing just that.' In fact, his enlistment was deferred for twelve months because of the value of the publicity work he was doing.

The first war poster Hilder designed was one for Defence Bonds. This was a colourful maritime picture of a view over the stern of a destroyer looking towards a convoy. The most telling part of the design was the white ensign fluttering from its jackstaff against an aquamarine sky. This poster was pasted all over the hoardings of Britain. The foot of Nelson's column in Trafalgar Square was surrounded by huge versions of the poster which was painted by the Harker Brothers' studio, the theatrical scene painters at the Bricklayers' Arms, south of Tower Bridge. These giant hand-painted posters were incorporated by Felix Topolski in his drawing *River Plate Victories in Trafalgar Square February 23 1940.*

Whilst waiting to be called up for the army, Hilder was continuing with his designs for Christmas cards for the Ward Gallery, was out recording the Sussex landscape for the Pilgrim Trust, and illustrating with very free pen drawings a book by L. A. G. Strong called *They went to the island.* Most of his time, however, was taken up with publicity work for the R.A.F.

TAILS UP!

1940 Press advertisement drawing for the R.A.F. recruiting campaign

1945 Advertisement drawing for Seven Seas Cod Liver Oil

Given 'em the slip this time!

1941 Illustration for *The Bible for Today,* Oxford, 1941. 'In the light of this revelation dare we go on building cities like this'

In January 1941, we visited the Hilders at Caterham. It was bitterly cold with snow on the ground. We found Rowland working on an R.A.F. drawing wrapped up in a fur coat. That night there was a terrrible raid on London. For most of the night we could hear the bombers thundering overhead and the intermittent clatter of anti-aircraft guns from the other side of Caterham.

In April Rowland Hilder was commissioned as a Camouflage Officer and posted to Farnham Castle for a six-weeks Camouflage course. He and Edith took a little eighteenth-century house in West Street, Farnham. The Camouflage training centre was commanded by a choleric old Etonian New Zealander called R. McLean Buckley. Dick Buckley was also a founder and the Honorary Secretary of the Royal Ocean Racing Club, so he had some sympathy for Hilder's interest in the sea, even though their kinds of yachting were so very different. The Camouflage Officers' Mess was run rather like a Senior Common Room. The Mess Secretary was Freddy Mayor, the owner of the Mayor Gallery in Cork Street. This gallery in the 1930s was the most *avant garde* in London, so Freddy Mayor was not exactly a supporter of Rowland Hilder's romantic evocation of the English countryside. Freddy

1936 Railway publicity pen and brush
drawings for LNER

c.1946 Drawing for use on a Heron Press envelope

was also a Machiavellian character. Hilder became something of a butt for his teasing humour. The fact that beneath Mayor's sharp barbs and bawdy wit was a very kindly man, was something that Rowland did not discover until it was too late to matter.

After the course was over he remained at Farnham Castle for some months. His talents were not wasted for he illustrated the standard *Army Manual on Camouflage* and did many instructional drawings. In the autumn he was posted to Chester and he could not have been unluckier. His immediate superior officer came of a titled family and was something of a Flashman character. Rowland Hilder never got his measure and he in turn never made any attempt to understand him. It was a most unhappy experience. As a result of all this, he became quite ill and eventually he was sent up before the Medical Board which, fortunately, proved to be both sensible and sympathetic. The Board's final recommendation was that Lieutenant R. Hilder should be released from the Army on medical grounds. The Brigadier who presided over this Board gave as his personal recommendation that Lieutenant Hilder's talents were being wasted and he would be better employed using them outside the army on behalf of the war effort. Just over twelve months from his being commissioned he was released from military service.

Whilst Rowland Hilder had been at Chester, Basil Spence, the architect, who was also a Camouflage Officer, had taken over the lease of the house in Farnham. The Spences gracefully relinquished it when the Hilders returned. Within days Rowland Hilder was working for the C.O.I. which he continued to do until the end of the war.

This war propaganda work consisted of posters, illustrations and drawings for press advertisements. He did a tremendous drawing of Liberty ships being built at the Kaiser shipyard in California. (This was propaganda for South America.) One of the most effective posters that he drew was one of an idyllic sunny summer landscape which inspired the composer Dr Ralph Vaughan Williams to write to him. He did a thundering great picture of battleships in line astern blazing into action (it looked more like Jutland than any naval engagement in the Hitler war) for a poster for the Middle East. He also drew posters of British shipbuilding and the covers of the official magazine *Envoy*. There is a particularly effective one of Tower Bridge (see pages 96 and 97).

The pastoral poster that had evoked the letter from Vaughan Williams resulted in George Rainbird, who was then a director of Holden's Advertising, approaching Hilder after the war had ended

1948 Snow scene for a Heron Press Christmas card. Watercolour drawing

1944 Propaganda poster for the Middle East,
with slogan set in Arabic

to ask him if he would paint a series of landscapes to be reproduced
in full colour as calendars and also as posters for the Brewing firm
of Whitbread. This once again was something new in advertising.
These were paintings reproduced for advertising, yet they were
paintings produced with an understanding of the needs of process
reproduction. They were not paintings, such as Sir John Millais's
Bubbles bought off the Royal Academy walls and adapted (with the
introduction of a cake of soap) for the purpose of advertising, nor
were they 'designed' posters in the sense that the landscape posters

From the Original by Rowland Hilder

TO ENJOY THE FRUITS OF VICTORY

∗ SAVE NOW ∗

1944 Poster for the National Savings Group.
'To enjoy the Fruits of Victory'

of such artists as Fred Taylor or E. McKnight Kauffer had been in the 1930s.

The scheme was most successful and Hilder was asked to complement the paintings with black and white drawings to be used for press advertising. He drew winter scenes and scenes of harvesting and orchards, haymaking and threshing. In these black and white drawings, Hilder was still using the rather formalized technique which he had used for *The Bible for Today*. This was the

1973 Winter landscape. Oil painting 28 × 40in. Reproduced by Royle
Publications as a large print and also as a Christmas card

engraver's technique of closely ruled lines to indicate tonal changes. The most effective pen drawing for these Whitbread advertisements was one of Kentish hopfields, which was reproduced to sizes as large as 9in high and as small as 3in high. These drawings had to be drawn in a technique which would stand up to this variable reduction.

By the time the Whitbread scheme was under way, the Hilders had returned to Kidbrooke Grove. There they started the Heron Press to market and publish Rowland Hilder's Christmas cards and prints. Rowland and his father ran the press and Lindsay Glegg, who had also been in Army Camouflage, was a sleeping partner and provided some financial guarantee, on which in fact they never had to call. Lindsay Glegg, played a useful part however, in introducing the Heron Press to his family printing firm, Alabaster Passmore. It was a time of severe paper shortage but the printers were helpful and by great good fortune the Heron Press was able to buy a million envelopes which had been intended for Russia. Mr Hilder (Rowland's father) had retired from his job at Siemens's and took over the marketing of the cards with enthusiasm and untiring energy. He travelled all over the country selling the cards. The result of this and because it was a seller's market meant that they sold every card that they produced. They prospered and, as a result of the success of the Whitbread scheme, Hilder was flooded with offers of work.

By 1951 'Rowland Hilder' was a household name and at Christmas time the Heron Press cards were again on every mantelpiece. Also a number of Hilder's paintings were being reproduced and sold as prints. He was still *the* popular landscape artist of the time. 1951 was the year of the Festival of Britain, yet Hilder was not asked to contribute. This was another of those paradoxes that had beset his career up to that time. His reputation with the general public had never been so high; with the establishment, that is the world of art critics and other arbiters of taste, it had never been so low. It was as if such popularity debarred an artist from serious consideration. No doubt the print makers of the past, the Alkens, the Daniells, the Cruikshanks, Rowlandson and so on were regarded, or more likely disregarded, in the same kind of way.

Three years later Rowland Hilder collaborated with his wife Edith on the *Shell Guide to Flowers of the Countryside*. This should have given the most hidebound of the establishment something to think about. These brilliant advertisements – Rowland Hilder designed them and painted the backgrounds, Edith Hilder painted the flowers and Geoffrey Grigson wrote the script – had the widest exposure any coloured advertisement drawings have ever had: over 9,000,000 every month.

1944 Drawing of the Kaiser Shipyard in the USA, for the Ministry of
Information. 18 × 30in

Um navio mercante ao ser lançado à água numa carreira naval britânica

A GRÃ-BRETANHA E A AMÉRICA TEEM HOJE EM DIA MAIS DE DOIS MILHÕES
DE TONELADAS DE NAVEGAÇÃO DO QUE TINHAM EM AGÔSTO DE 1942

Serviço de Imprensa e Informação da Embaixada Británica

1944 Propaganda poster for South America

1944 Cover of propaganda magazine *Envoy*

1955 Sketch for 'January' from *The Shell
Guide to Flowers of the Countryside*

Vernon Nye of Shell was the architect of the scheme and George
Rainbird was the impresario. It was the biggest advertising scheme
ever launched in this country. The pictures went on exhibition and
toured the whole of the United States. They were reproduced as
wall charts for schools and finally published in book form by
Phoenix House. Immense pains were taken not only by the Hilders

1955 'April' from *The Shell Guide to Flowers of the Countryside*, drawn
and painted by Rowland and Edith Hilder. $21\frac{1}{2} \times 20$in

1955 Detailed study for 'March' from *The Shell Guide to Flowers of the Countryside* by Rowland and Edith Hilder

1943 Edith Hilder. Drawing in line and wash. 11 × 8in

and Grigson but also by the various botanists they consulted to make sure the pictures were not only lovely to look at but also botanically correct, down to the smallest detail. Vernon Nye warned the Hilders, 'Any mistakes and we shall get 10,000 letters a month pointing them out.'

The wild flowers were followed up in due course with other schemes. The first was the *Shell Guide to Counties*. Hilder initiated the scheme with a drawing of Kent; the remaining counties were done by other artists more or less successfully. The last Shell scheme Rowland was involved in was one of *Bird Sanctuaries* for which he drew a marshland view of Minsmere, a subject close to his heart.

In 1958 the Hilders moved to St Julian's, near Sevenoaks, to join an experiment in community living. For the previous couple of years they had had a room there which they used as a weekend studio. A printing press was set up and they called it the Rumshott Press. The intention was to print and market the Heron cards. Rowland's father, who was finding the work a strain, relinquished the cards. He remained at Blackheath but still dealt with the large prints. This experiment in living, though interesting, did not work. Two years later they were back in Kidbrooke Grove.

1965 Painting of Minsmere for the *Shell Guide to Bird Sanctuaries.*
20 × 30in

1958 Painting to illustrate the *Shell Guide to Kent.* This was the first of a
series of advertisement drawings done by a number of different artists.
20 × 30in

1959 Christmas card for the GPO commemorating fifty years of ship to
shore wireless service

1960 'The Royal Eagle'. Publicity design for Shell Petroleum Company.
This design is based on drawings done in the 1920s

1958 'The Soho Wharf at Burton-upon-Trent'. Christmas card for Bass and Worthington

In 1960 the colour printing and publishing firm of Royle approached Hilder. Rowland Hilder had met Ralph Royle when their respective sons, Anthony and Jeremy, were at school at Frensham Heights. As a result of their discussions, Royle took over the stock of the Heron Press and agreed to distribute the cards. Meanwhile anything Rowland painted they would reproduce either as fine prints or for Christmas cards. The arrangement worked so smoothly that in 1963 Royle took over the Heron Press and Hilder became a director of the firm. Royle's consultant art director was Noel Carrington and he must have played a part in these negotiations. In the previous three years Hilder had learned much of what Carrington was doing for the firm and when Carrington retired in 1963 Hilder assumed his responsibilities and became art adviser to Royle.

Rowland Hilder's career as a commercial illustrator had virtually ended. It had been a long road, but from this time onwards all he had to do was to paint. The fact that many of these paintings were going to be reproduced was incidental. The advances in graphic reproduction since the end of the war had been so great that no longer did the artist have to falsify or overstate his colours and tones to achieve any kind of result. The scanners could pick up anything that was on paper or canvas. The painting could now be an end in itself.

1972 Stamp book cover design, one of a series of four drawings of well-known ships

Part 3

1. How the artist works

In the 1960s Rowland Hilder wrote a little book called *Starting with Watercolour* which had considerable sales in both the USA and Great Britain.[1] It was a refreshingly simple book that gives one a very good idea of how an artist such as Hilder approaches his work. The book is full of sound, practical advice. It is devoid of art jargon, yet it is also mercifully unlike most of the so-called 'How-to-do-it' art books. Hilder starts the book by talking about drawing. He writes: 'You learn to draw by continuing to draw ... Begin to draw fearlessly with something that will make a clear black line. Draw the things around you: the room, the table laid for a meal, the view from the window. If you draw a line in the wrong place, make a correction on the same drawing, with a bolder, firm line. At all costs keep going, even if the efforts do not seem impressive. When you are puzzled as to how to proceed, look at the reproductions of the masters. Make free-hand copies of their works. Find out and understand how they put a drawing together, and above all what they leave out.'

Hilder takes the student through exercises in drawing in line, pencil, pen and brush and charcoal and on white and toned papers and he gives some useful hints on perspective. Hilder could indeed have carved a successful career as an architectural draughtsman. The drawings of Canterbury and Staithes on page 168 are really quite remarkable examples of such drawing. In his book he explains how the perspective of a drawing like the one of Staithes is done. The almost impossible problem for a beginner of working out how the perspective works when doing a drawing of a street that is sloping away downhill and yet to keep the houses from looking as if they were falling into the sea. Where the sea meets the sky is of course the horizon and Hilder suggests that a pin is stuck into this horizon. A ruler is then laid against it to act as a guide for the projection of the roof lines of the house. It is a simple elementary expedient, yet without it the student would be quite lost.

Various hints and recipes give one many insights into Hilder's own methods. For instance the basic palette he suggests for outside sketching is limited to the simple range of lamp black, burnt sienna, yellow ochre and cobalt blue.

The book is studded with little thumbnail sketches (in fact when executed they would be about 7 × 5in.) It is in this form that he brings the work back to the studio when he has been out sketching.

He describes in the foreword the kind of nonsensical rules that the 'purist' watercolourist worked under, such as 'You must not use opaque colour' or 'You must not use pen or conté pencil.' 'In fact', he summarizes, 'you must not indulge in any procedure that

[1] *Starting with Watercolour*, Rowland Hilder. Published in New York by Watson Guptill and in London by Studio Vista, 1966.

1976 Rowland Hilder sketching at Shoreham, Kent, *Photograph: Rado Klose*

1871 'The Pool of London'. Etching by James McNeill Whistler 5⅜ × 8⅜in

departs from the strict definition of pure watercolour.' He gradually discards these fatuities, at length throwing them into the trash can where they deserve to be consigned. As he says: 'The visual experiences which really excited me seemed to call for a more flexible means of expression. When I tried to paint moving white sails of boats at Cowes Regatta, I found it impossible to capture the scene by following the advice which involved painting a transparent watercolour sky and leaving the sails as the natural white of the paper. The yachts had moved away before the first wash was dry! By experiment I found that I got very much what I needed by painting the sails in opaque white body colour on tinted paper.' Having disobeyed the rules of the pundits he then discovered, when looking at the Turner sketches in the Print Room of the British Museum, that the master had followed exactly the same procedure.

Whistler's Thames etchings were an early influence on Rowland Hilder's work and in fact provide the jumping-off point for more than one of his later paintings. Whistler has in fact been a lasting inspiration to his work as a marine artist. When, as a young man, Hilder used to hire a sailing boat and sail up to Limehouse and the Port of London, bits of Whistler's Thames-side were still standing, though most of the remaining old houses were pulled down in the early 1920s. Only the Prospect of Whitby has survived. Today it is a tourist attraction; in those days it was just a waterside pub.

1976 Waterside houses, Pool of London. Watercolour inspired by details
in Whistler's Thames etchings 10 × 15in

1937 The Prospect of Whitby. Pen drawing 4 × 7in

1975 Boys watching television at Twinstead. Line and watercolour
$6\frac{1}{2} \times 9$in. *Henry Stucke Esq*

The drawings of the boys watching television and painting were
done at Twinstead in Essex. Hilder does a lot of sketches of people.
He does this as a form of relaxation. It is interesting to note the
simple use of counter change to reveal the two boys' faces. Both
the medium and the manner of drawing is that used by Rembrandt,
whose economy of statement, as in the sketch opposite, had a
profound influence on Hilder's later works.

1975 Boys sketching at Twinstead.
Line and watercolour $6\frac{1}{2} \times 9$in

c.1650 Landscape by Rembrandt. Pen and
wash in bistre. 'The bend of the Amstel'. *Louvre
Museum*

These two sketches by Rembrandt, of the Amstel river and the boy
pulling a rope, were drawn with a pen and brush, using diluted inks
and bistre, which is a pigment made from wood ash.

In most of Turner's sketches, the darker tones were drawn or
painted on a tonal background and the lights were added in chalk,
pastel, gouache or other light-toned media. In talking about this
approach, Hilder said: 'Turner prepared his sketch books by
tinting his paper with watercolour washes of grey-blue, cream or
buff, so did Constable. He would select from his sketch book a
background colour suitable to the atmosphere of the day; he would
draw the outline and darker areas in pen or pencil – adding washes
for half tones that were darker than the background – then
indicating the whites and lighter areas in chalk or in solid body
colour or light washes of the same. The choice of background tone
and colour will set the tone and colour key of the picture to be
painted. It really is such a simple method, but you must think it out
first. I remember one of my instructors saying "Pictures can go
wrong before they are painted". Time spent in thinking and
planning is repaid with interest. For instance a key can be too high
or too low to convey the mood of the subject!

'The actual scenes in nature are very complicated and pictorially
confusing. One has to simplify and reject anything irrelevant and
also anything that may weaken the impact of one's statement. It is
much easier to paint in low tones. If one starts in too high a key
there is nothing to differentiate between the tones in the upper
register. One cannot paint a lighter tone than white so that only
white can register as a lighter tone than the background. Thus we
have to make do with pure white for clouds, weather-boarded mills,
yachts, gulls and so on. By dropping the tone key one can show
differences between these light objects.' The experiments overleaf
were done quite recently as demonstrations to show students a
method of making rapid tonal sketches from nature.

c. 1650 'Young man pulling a rope' by
Rembrandt: Pen and wash in bistre $11\frac{3}{8} \times 7$in

Looking at the Turner sketches confirmed Hilder's tentative ideas and showed him that Turner had made any medium his servant and on that evidence there was no place for stupid dogma.

The first experiment (opposite) is based on one of Turner's sketches of Rouen. In this copy, Hilder tried to show the use of the traditional method of tonal painting as a means of indicating a full tone scale even in the slightest preliminary sketch. Turner's original was done on a blue-grey (rather faded) sugar paper using a warm sepia line with grey-blue washes for sky and water and with the addition of washes of white body colour warmed by a little ochre.

The second experiment (above) is a loose-transcription of a detail of the same Turner sketch and of a sketch by the East Anglian painter Henry Bright of Thorpe Meadows with Norwich in the distance. Rowland Hilder has simplified the sketches using a black wash strengthened with a 2B carbon pencil. The light tones in the sky, which are reflected in the water, were added with white body colour.

Opposite:
1964 Studies after one of Turner's sketches of Rouen and a sketch by Henry Bright of Thorpe Meadows, Norwich. Watercolour $10 \times 6\frac{1}{2}$in

c.1833 Sketch of Rouen on toned paper by J. W. M. Turner. Reproduced from Turner's sketch

1964 Study after Turner's sketch of Rouen 7×5in

n.d. 'Thorpe Meadows with Norwich in Distance' by Henry Bright. Chalk on buff paper. *Castle Museum, Norwich.*

c.1833 Three pencil sketches on tinted paper
by J. W. M. Turner. Reproduced from *Turner's
Colour Sketches 1820-34*

1977 'Windy Day'. Watercolour after Turner sketches $5\frac{1}{4} \times 10\frac{1}{4}$in

The three sketches by Turner on the opposite page were drawn in
black, white and red chalk on a brown paper. The subjects are a
scene on a beach with sailing boats, steam boats and breaking seas.
It is not known if Turner ever painted any pictures from these
notes. It was on this slight basis that Rowland Hilder did the little
watercolour of *Windy Day* above. Hilder's action in doing this is
comparable to a composer like Britten developing a theme by
Purcell.

Throughout Rowland Hilder's working life, drawing has provided
the keystone to his work. Again and again he goes back to nature
to recharge his batteries. If he is not drawing oast houses and
ploughed fields, boats and saltings, then he is sketching the people
round him. He is a *compulsive* draughtsman and ultimately by his
drawing I think his work will be judged.

1968 Malta. Watercolour sketch $6\frac{1}{2} \times 9$in

1968 Malta. Tone study of waves. $6\frac{1}{2} \times 9$in

1968 Malta looking towards Rabat. Watercolour $6\frac{1}{2} \times 9$in

In these tonal studies of Malta the artist is putting into actual use the experiments on the previous pages. The study of waves is on a blue toned paper, drawn in ink and gouache.

Overleaf:
These pages from Rowland Hilder's sketchbooks show different aspects of his work. The study of the huge cedar of Lebanon was made at Frensham Heights when his daughter Mary was at school there. The oast houses and ricks have been drawn in carbon pencil and wash. This drawing, like the other two on this page, were done on tinted paper.

The carbon pencil study of the bank of trees was drawn from the library window at Tyringham, a health cure farm he was visiting.

When actually working out of doors, Rowland Hilder works rapidly, as he tries to capture the whole scene rather than to make an accurate drawing. He often works on tinted paper with carbon pencil, washes of lamp black and white body colour. His aim in such atmospheric pictures is to achieve simple relationships of flat areas of tone, comparable to the paintings of John Sell Cotman. His methods are the traditional ones of the English masters, painting on a toned background, working in pencil, conté, chalk, ink and even in oil paint on paper.

1960 Study of a tree. Watercolour $4\frac{1}{2} \times 7\frac{1}{2}$in

1950 Study of ricks and oast houses. Pencil and wash $5\frac{1}{2} \times 7\frac{1}{2}$in

1973 Study of trees. Carbon pencil and watercolour 7×10in

Such early studies as these of the warehouses by Rochester Bridge and the period motor vehicles outside a timber yard at Whitstable have provided the foundations of Rowland Hilder's later work. His early drawings become in time a part of his present work, though over the years he may have discarded much along the way. He has used them for references and as the starting point for new paintings.

1929 Barges alongside warehouses by
Rochester Bridge. Watercolour $7\frac{3}{4} \times 10\frac{1}{4}$ in

1932 Wood's Yard, Whitstable. Pencil and
wash $7 \times 8\frac{1}{2}$ in

The first sketch shown here was drawn during
the 1939–45 War near Farnham in Surrey with
a carbon pencil on a piece of buff paper. A soft
lead pencil was used for the tones.

The sketch of trees and a shallow river was
drawn with a sharpened matchstick dipped in
Indian ink (he had left his pen at home). The
washes are in burnt sienna and lamp black.
After this experiment Rowland Hilder often
used a sharpened stick for drawing in ink. He
found it more flexible than a pen. The portrait
of his wife on page 100 is done in this way.

The sketch of farm buildings and a rick (one of
the buildings was a camouflaged pill box) was
drawn on the ruled sheet of a pocket notebook
during an army exercise in 1942. It was done
at Tilford in Surrey and the actual sketch was
much the same size as the reproduction here.

The sketch of boats and the canal at Chioggia was drawn in black pen line with sepia, ochre and burnt sienna washes.

The sketch of the Thames was rather larger than the others on these two pages, which were mostly about 5 × 7in. It was made whilst the artist was sitting on the deck of a lighter which he had boarded from his sailing punt.

The drawing of church and park land was made with black and brown marker pens on thin bank paper.

1967 Ruined barns. Line and watercolour 6½ × 9in

This very free watercolour sketch of ruined barns was done in a lane on the border of Kent and Sussex. Hilder has more than once returned to the area, but has failed to find the barns. He thinks they may have been pulled down.

The sketch of the shed and chickens was done in carbon pencil and wash. It was a quick note to provide material for a later painting. It was drawn in the Isles of Scilly.

The use of a camera by painters often strikes those who are not artists as being slightly reprehensible. David Hockney, a painter whose work may seem poles apart from Hilder's, in fact parallels Hilder's remarks at many points and discusses his work in the same down-to-earth manner. About the use of photography Hockney says:

'I use photographs for reference; it is difficult to paint from photographs. If you haven't taken the photograph yourself you can only do something imaginative with it. If you took it, at least you can remember you are only using it to jog your memory, make a note of a shape. To draw from photographs is impossible I think, they don't have enough information.'

1958 Shed with corrugated iron roof. Bryher, Isles of Scilly. Carbon pencil and wash 7 × 10in

Hilder says: 'I use a camera for gathering information but as the camera's eye is quite different from the human eye, I find photographs useful just for this one thing. I may take twenty photographs for one picture. The one thing you cannot do is to learn to draw from photographs and as for trying to paint from colour photographs ... what is the point of trying to paint from a Kodachrome, the painting will look just like a Kodachrome unless you are a Hockney. You can then transmute the photographic dross if you are clever enough into gold. It has provided you with a launching pad.' He continued on this photographic theme, 'There is nothing new about artists using photographs. Corot used them widely, the Impressionists were the first to make good use of them. Degas found Muybridge's action photographs transformed the way he saw things (not the way he painted); Manet used them for likenesses, the Pre-Raphaelites used them for detailed reference; Millais commissioned Beatrix Potter's father to take photographs not only of some of his sitters but also of landscapes; Degas introduced Sickert to the use of photographs and so on ...'

'The upshot of all this is that photography can be a very useful tool in the hands of an artist who knows what he is looking for. Whether he uses it as an *aide memoire* for likenesses, details,

1966 Photograph of farm yard

1966 Photograph of fields and oast houses, Kent

1966 Farm yard. Watercolour $7\frac{1}{4} \times 10\frac{1}{4}$ in

backgrounds and so on or whether he uses it as a starting point, as Sickert did and as the Pop artists such as Rauschenberg did, or as Hockney does, is up to them. One thing is certain, all these chaps have learned their job first. Give a student a camera before he has learned to draw and the odds are he never will draw. And if he can't draw he has not learned to use his eyes so he is not in business.'

These photographs taken by Anthony Hilder for his father show some indication of possible uses either for reference or as a starting point for a picture. The landscape of a farm near Shoreham might conceivably serve as a starting point for a painting, though it leaves much for the artist to add.

The two photographs from different angles of a farmyard in the north-east of Kent could certainly be used for reference, particularly if you wanted to draw a tractor. That one of these could provide the beginnings for a picture does not seem very likely, but Hilder has taken from the second photograph the basic forms of the two barns and the hedgerow trees in the background and has produced this little sketch, which in itself could well be the basis of a painting.

1966 Photograph of the same farm

1976 Woodbridge: low water. Watercolour $5\frac{1}{2} \times 7\frac{1}{2}$in (after a photograph by Bob Alcock)

1976 Ketch beating up the Stour (detail).
Watercolour sketch $7\frac{1}{2} \times 5\frac{1}{2}$in

The perennial question that is put to most artists is:
'How do pictures start?'
On the next three pages are three of Rowland Hilder's different starting points: they are:
1 From photographs
2 From the subconscious
3 From lines or plans or other technical information

The watercolour sketch of the Woodbridge river at low water was inspired by a photograph taken by Bob Alcock. This photograph was used for the jacket of a book I had written called *A Taste for Sailing*. The photograph did little more than provide an idea for the composition, yet the mood of the photograph evoked a string of memories. The freedom of the sketch is based on many years of actually drawing such scenes and could never have developed solely by working from the photographs.

1974 Conference doodle. Pen on drawing pad cover $6\frac{1}{2} \times 8$in

The drawing on the cover of a pad of Phase II Recycled Paper came
from nowhere! It was doodled during a business conference in the
USA whilst discussing matters quite remote from the subjects
drawn here. The artist said, 'There was no reason for doing it, it
was just a piece of unconscious expression.' The subject is of
course one near to his heart. Though it has not done so, so far, it
could well provide the idea for a painting.

The study of a small ketch beating up an estuary was one of several
sketches made for a projected illustrated edition of a book about
sailing that had more than a mutual interest for both of us. The
information about the boat came from a set of lines, a sail plan, a
photograph and the fact that I had told the artist that the sails
were tanned and the boat was painted black. This is an example of
converting the bare facts of plans etc, into a living picture.

1976 Sloten: Friesland. Watercolour sketch $5\frac{1}{2} \times 7\frac{1}{2}$in

The drawings in the sketch-book pad were suggested by two of the author's photographs but are of course based on a lengthy acquaintance with such Dutch windmills, canals and harbours.

The sketch of the barge and a warehouse is quite a different thing. It is merely using the sketch-book to record ideas as opposed to drawing something or a scene that is in front of the artist. Such a sketch is made from half-remembered scenes. He almost leaves it to his hand to wander across the paper and let the scene develop of its own volition.

1977 Rowland Hilder in his studio at Blackheath. *Photograph: Rado Klose*

1973 Study of barge unloading. $5\frac{1}{2} \times 7\frac{1}{2}$in

1932 Glue factory on the Swale. Watercolour with carbon pencil 15 × 20in

1932 Canvey Island bridge. Watercolour with carbon pencil 8¾ × 12¼in

1965 Yachts on the hard: West Mersea. Watercolour 14 × 20in

The drawing of the glue factory, which was beside the Swale near Queenborough, is quite an early work. These old clapboard buildings were pulled down many years ago. The picture is typical of this period when Hilder relied very much on the quality of his draughtsmanship to give substance to his subject. The use of the contrasting simple flat washes is an effective counterfoil to the drawing.

The conté pencil and wash drawing of a flimsy wooden bridge joining Canvey Island to the mainland, like much of Rowland Hilder's early work, shows the influence of Muirhead Bone, particularly in the precise drawing of the piles that support the structure.

The watercolour of yachts on the hard at West Mersea is in some contrast to the watercolour drawings opposite. It was done some thirty years after those two drawings. The view is one looking down river towards the Bradwell Power Station. In the middle distance to the right is Packing Shed Island. Drawing is still part and parcel of Hilder's technique, but by this time he had become more interested in the play of light on the clouds and the water and even on the wet shingly foreshore.

1946 Boston Cut: high water. Watercolour 15 × 20in

This watercolour was done over thirty years ago. It shows the approach to Boston from the Wash, with the famous Boston Stump rising up behind the houses to the left of the picture. The other watercolour, done at the same time, is of the river at low water. Rowland Hilder's assurance as an architectural draughtsman is shown in these two pictures. The precision of the drawing of the fishing smack and of the tall warehouses behind it establishes a belief in the picture as a whole, even though the rest of the buildings are represented in the simplest of terms.

In both of these pictures, which were drawn on the spot, the artist was looking into the light. The treatment of the water is very simple: in the painting of the Boston Cut at low water it was represented by just two contrasting tones, light in the foregound, dark as the river passes between the buildings. The treatment of the boats resting on the mud is little more than a series of very free notes, yet they read and are more than adequate. In fact, as can be seen in the detail picture, the sailing barge, sitting firmly on its flat bottom is a brilliantly economic statement.

1946 Boston Cut: low water. Watercolour 15 × 20in

1946 Detail from the painting above of a sailing barge sitting on the mud

1958 Oast houses near Faversham. Watercolour
on Whatman heavy rough surface paper 20 × 30in

Hilder has done two watercolour versions of this view. The one
here was painted in early spring and the other in early summer
when the trees were in blossom.

Part 3

2. The Rowland Hilder landscape

By 1963 Rowland Hilder was at last free to paint. Of course he had been painting throughout his career, but such painting that he did was always overshadowed not so much by his commercial illustration as by his role as a print maker. Print making can mean more than the making of autographical prints, by whatever process they may be done. It can and does mean photographic reproductions of drawings and paintings. For the first half of the twentieth century the process was often imperfect and artists had to compensate for it in various ways. This meant that the actual painting was not an end in itself; in fact it mattered little providing the reproduction was all right.

From the 1960s onwards Hilder was liberated from such constrictions and over the next few years he achieved a means of expression that was a striking advance on everything he had done before. It was of course built on a lifetime's experience of drawing and looking at things, yet he was still lumbered with the role of 'the popular artist', whether he liked it or not.

In spite of the fact that he left the United States of America when he was only ten years old, he paints like an American. He is much closer to such an artist as Andrew Wyeth than he is to any contemporary English painter. The English landscape painter tends to be much more restrained than his American counterpart. There is a tendency, because of their preoccupation with tone as opposed to colour, to produce rather murky little pictures. Fredrick Gore, writing a few years ago, said: 'Tone has been the bug-bear of British art . . . French theory does not admit tone as having a separate existence from colour, the London Schools have always encouraged painting accurate differences of tone in any colour, hence good old Slade mud.'[2] Hilder has had his preoccupations and his problems with tone. As he started as a chiaroscuro draughtsman the tone was built into the drawing. Over the years he has slowly shed this framework and tone has become inseparable from the colour.

One of the turning points in his development as a painter occured when he discovered the value of underpainting with acrylic paints. He began using this particular method in about 1965, by which time acrylic paints had been perfected and proven. Acrylic paint does have practical advantages for underpainting. Unlike oil paint, which slowly over the years continues to oxydize and to go yellow with age, acrylic paint dries hard, quickly and right down to the canvas and the colour and medium remain constant, as far as one knows, for ever.

[2] Introduction by Frederick Gore ARA to the Catalogue of John Nash's Retrospective Exhibition at the Royal Academy of Arts, 1967.

1970 Oast houses near Box Hill in winter 10 × 13½in

At a recent exhibition of his work some lady asked Hilder 'How long did that painting take you to do?' The artist looked a bit thoughtful and then said: 'Fifty-three years.' The questioner was dumbfounded, so he put her mind at rest by saying, 'I did a first sketch of that when I was barely more than a student. Over the years I went back to that place but it never looked the same, anyhow they had pulled down most of the buildings. I had a shot at doing a painting of it and it did not come off. Over the years I must have taken innumerable stabs at it, then at last it came right – the final painting was spread over a couple of months. It is what I saw all those years ago and it has taken me until now to be able to realize it.' There was a silence while his questioner was trying to think of something to say when Hilder brought the conversation to a close by saying: 'I expect you think I am a very slow worker.'

The watercolour of oast houses near Box Hill was painted with a very simple palette of washes of lamp black and the earth colours burnt sienna, burnt umber and yellow ochre.

The little scribble in the margin was made on the back of an envelope not much larger than the reproduction. It was the basis of the oil study at the foot of the opposite page and was done just before the oasts were converted into a house.

Both the pictures on the opposite page are studies. The one above is a watercolour detail for the Shoreham picture overleaf, the one below is a study in oil for yet another painting of the Chiddingstone oast houses.

1976 Study of oast houses near Chiddingstone.
Pen drawing 3 × 4¼in

1976 Detail study for painting of farm near Shoreham. Watercolour 10 × 15in

1977 Study of oast houses at Chiddingstone. Oil on canvas 24 × 36in

1976 Hop fields and oast houses near Chiddingstone. Watercolour
20 × 30in

1965 Kentish farm, near Shoreham. Watercolour 20 × 36in

This panoramic picture of a Kentish farm is based on a view near Shoreham in Kent. The great thatched barn shown here was painted by Samuel Palmer. Rowland Hilder had drawn it just before it was demolished and replaced with a practical but most unromantic Dutch barn.

The way Rowland Hilder works is quite unlike the methods used by a topographical draughtsman who sets his easel up in front of a place and records it. What Hilder does is to walk over his landscape, to view it from a hundred different viewpoints, to sketch it from half a dozen places and to photograph it from every possible angle. This is the basic material which he mulls over, boils down and finally synthesizes. In the collecting of information, some of the sketches may hit on the essence of the subject, but most do not. But like the photographs they may still provide some useful detail or facet.

The watercolour drawing of the oast houses at Chiddingstone is drawn on French Canson deep-toned buff paper. The painting is in the tradition of the East Anglian painters John Crome or Henry Bright. The buff paper gives it the warmth of old varnish.

1977 Hop fields and oast houses near Shoreham, Kent. Watercolour
$9\frac{3}{4} \times 13\frac{1}{2}$in

The watercolour of the hop fields and oast houses near Shoreham is of a scene looking towards Otford. It was drawn on the spot, the artist sitting in his car with his pad propped up against the steering wheel. The tones of this drawing were put in with grey, buff and brown marker pens, then later on in the studio the sky was added in gouache. The trees were then painted in waterproof casein paint so that the artist could run watercolour washes over their deep tones. It is a fresh and pretty picture.

Rowland Hilder is first of all a watercolour painter. For some reason watercolour painting in England has always been considered a less important medium than oil painting (as if it mattered what an artist painted in!). This is certainly not a viewpoint subscribed to in America. Andrew Wyeth, like Hilder, is also primarily a watercolour painter, following in the tradition of artists like Winslow Homer. There is another point of similarity between Rowland Hilder and the younger Wyeth and that is that Hilder's landscapes are rarely peopled 'yet his pictures always show a trace of man' – what Anthony Quinton referred to as 'My ideal landscape, without people, but with clear signs of elemental life.'[3]

Yet another thing Hilder shares with the American artist is the clear hard light that illuminates so many of his winter landscapes. It's like theatre lighting in its intensity.

[3] BBC World Service *Letter from London*, 1975.

1975 Kentish Weald. Watercolour sketch $7\frac{1}{4} \times 5\frac{1}{4}$in

1975 Notebook sketch. Watercolour 7×10in

1975 Fill dyke. Watercolour 15 × 20in

1975 Ploughed field. Watercolour $7\frac{1}{4} \times 10\frac{3}{4}$in

1975 Panorama of Buckinghamshire. Watercolour $7\frac{1}{4} \times 10\frac{3}{4}$in

Paintings are built up on an accumulation of data allied to a lifetime's experience. Making notes and doing small sketches is a preliminary to any picture that Hilder paints. The sketch above, in itself quite small, was painted from thumbnail notes made whilst the artist was staying at a health cure farm at Tyringham in Buckinghamshire. In fact it was done in the middle of a nine-day fast! It is an autumnal scene, with the inevitable burning of leaves in the middle distance. The low-register colour scheme, with the foreground almost in silhouette, was to show the effect of light in a cloudy sky. It was drawn in a sketch-book on Bockingford paper, a soft, cheap paper which is not suitable for works intended to be permanent.

The two quite small watercolour drawings opposite were the result of a winter's day walk over rain-soaked fields near Twinstead in Suffolk Wet plough-land or a water-logged cart track might not strike the layman as likely subjects for a painter. By working against the wintry sun, the artist has succeeded in filling the paintings with light.

In his winter landscapes of deserted ploughed fields, Hilder communicates a sense of how small man is in contrast to nature. Richard McLanathan writing, about Andrew Wyeth, said: 'There is a Thoreau-like sense of place in Andrew Wyeth's work.'[4] This is equally true of Hilder's landscapes. People are always saying to

[4] Introduction to the catalogue of *The Brandywine Heritage* exhibition.

1975 Mid-Suffolk: Constable's Country. Watercolour $7\frac{1}{4} \times 10\frac{3}{4}$in

1975 Notebook sketch. Watercolour 7×10in

1975 Sussex lane. Watercolour $7\frac{1}{4} \times 10\frac{3}{4}$in

him, 'I know that lane, or that clump of elms so well.' In fact he never paints with any kind of topographical intent. What he is painting is the mood or the feeling that such landscapes give him. The lane or the clump of elms is any Kentish lane or any clump of Sussex elms.

The watercolour of the Sussex lane was drawn during one of two fine days in mid-March, the days that each year Hilder relies on for drawing out of doors. 'These fine days', so he said, 'seem to recur with remarkable regularity.' The trees are drawn in warm colours, raw umber, burnt umber and brown ink, over a pale blue watercolour sky. The distant trees are a warm purplish grey.

The two sketches on the opposite page are of East Anglia, the top is of a view near the head of one of the estuaries, the lower of the Constable Country, with Constable very much in mind. The bronze green that Hilder used in this sketch is the one that Constable used for paintings of high summer; it is made up of lamp black and permanent yellow.

The notebook sketches on these pages have been chosen at random. The one with the leafless elms is to show the effects of the changing light of sun and showers, and the feeling of movement in the sky. The artist conveys the ephemeral quality of the scene. The sketch at the top of page 139 – the scene in the Weald – is an

1974 *Autumn*. Oil on canvas by Rowland and Edith Hilder. 24 × 36in

exercise in achieving distance, with a low horizon, by the use of receding tones. The heavy sky, loaded with rain, dominates the picture.

It is a rare thing nowadays for two artists to collaborate on one picture, but it would be a great pity if the collaboration between Rowland and Edith Hilder that proved so successful in the *Shell Guide to Flowers of the Countryside* was allowed to lapse. Though both of them are fully absorbed in their own work, once in a while they come together as in the painting *Autumn,* which has the same theme as the *November* painting they did for the Shell book. The pattern of working remains the same. They discuss the general scheme of the picture, Edith suggests what kind of flowers, berries or foliage would fit in with the time of year. Rowland does a charcoal rough sketch, Edith draws out her flowers, vegetation, etc. Then Rowland paints his landscape and Edith finally draws and paints her part. It is impossible to tell where one begins and the other leaves off.

These two sketches done against the light are almost Turneresque in the treatment of their skies. They were painted near Rowland Hilder's studio at Shellness on the Isle of Sheppey.

1975 Windmill on Isle of Sheppey. Watercolour sketch $5\frac{1}{4} \times 7\frac{1}{4}$in

1975 Pond and Marshes. Isle of Sheppey. Watercolour sketch $5\frac{1}{4} \times 7\frac{1}{4}$in

The watercolour of Cley Mill was taken from a small sketch done many years ago, drawn to show how the situation of the mill has changed, because of the protection of new sea walls. However, on a recent visit Rowland Hilder and his son Anthony found the marshes flooded once again. This was due to a very high spring tide and a north-westerly gale. Hilder made a rough gouache sketch of the mill, then later he returned to the mill to make notes of how it looked in the evening light. The sun had dropped below the horizon and there was a barely perceptible crescent moon. It was this that inspired the painting on page 148. He did another small colour sketch and when he returned home, photographed it on to 35mm film. This was projected on to the 24 × 36in canvas on which he had already painted the background sky. The projection of the mill was outlined on the canvas with a sharpened piece of charcoal, and where great precision was needed, as in the case of the windmill's sails, with a finely sharpened carbon pencil. The reason for using charcoal and carbon pencil is that they clean off easily and will in fact wash off. Lead pencil smears.

Rowland Hilder shares with the American painters of the Brandywine country 'An American extravagance in the intensity of their vision'[5]. His is an emotional art, a gut-reaction. He has indeed followed Howard Pyle's advice to his pupils: 'Throw your heart into the picture then jump in after it . . . feel the wind and rain on your skin when you paint it.'[6]

Like American illustrator-painters, such as Winslow Homer, Frederic Remington and William Glackens, Hilder has suffered from the denigration of illustration by contemporary critics, as if the fact of being a successful illustrator should automatically discount anyone's abilities as an artist.

In *The Nature and Aesthetics of Design* David Pye writes something very relevant to this attitude. 'That the artist should work in the general style of his time is all but inevitable, except in rare cases of men of exceptional powers.' Hilder is one of these rare cases; his exceptional powers can not be doubted. That his manner of painting is Pre-Impressionist is not a matter of chance or ignorance of all that has happened since the first *Salon des Refusés* exhibition in 1874 where Monet, Renoir and other like-thinking painters showed their work. The traditional methods of drawing and watercolour painting provided Hilder with the best medium

[5] The Brandywine country refers to painters and illustrators, such as Howard Pyle, N. C. Wyeth and his son Andrew, who all worked in that area. See *The Brandywine Heritage,* published in 1971 by the Brandywine River Museum, Chadd's Ford, Pennsylvania.

[6] *Ibid.*

1975 Cley Mill. Watercolour sketch 7 × 10in

1975 Cley Mill. Watercolour sketch $5\frac{1}{2} \times 7\frac{1}{2}$in

1975 Cley Mill. Watercolour 15 × 20in

for what he wanted to say. With his great skills as a draughtsman, he would have been wasting his talents if he had tried to express what he had to say by the Impressionist techniques of broken colour and flickering line. His concepts were clearly defined and he defined them by line and tone. Such interest as he had with light was to use it to reveal the basic forms. The fact that he has consistently limited his subject matter to the English landscape and seascape is not to imply that he is any less of an artist. On the contrary, such self-enforced limitations have meant that he has channelled all his powers into these two areas and so brought that much more intensity to his paintings.

To revert to Hilder's beginnings as an illustrator, some might think that only a genius could have survived such a beginning. In fact Sickert refuted such a suggestion when he wrote in reference to Turner and to Charles Keene, who both worked as hack illustrators when they were young. 'There is no greater mistake than to say that he [Turner] survived this because he was a genius. It is the other way about . . . [likewise] Keene learnt his trade "on the job", doing drawings for a threepenny comic paper to make a living. It was on this diet that he became one of the master draughtsmen of the world.'[7]

These may seem extravagant claims, but Sickert knew what he was talking about. The fact that the term 'illustrator' had become a derogatory term, he considered a nonsense and in fact said that he regarded himself as an illustrator, 'as', so he said, 'were all the greatest painters from Tintoretto to Turner'.[8]

[7] *The Life and Opinions of Walter Richard Sickert,* Robert Emmons, Faber, 1941.

[8] *Ibid.*

1976 The Swale. Watercolour $7\frac{1}{4} \times 10\frac{1}{4}$ in

Part 3

3. Marine painting

In his paintings of the sea Rowland Hilder shares a certain attitude not only with American painters but also with the American author Herman Melville. It is an attitude common to seamen, of regarding the sea as a great and elemental force. This is of course something that Turner had in full measure.

The watercolour of the Swale was painted from Hilder's Shellness studio window, using binoculars, following the practice of W. L. Wyllie, who in his studio on the Hoo Marshes had a powerful telescope, through which he could see shipping in both Thames and Medway. The three barges in this picture are at anchor, awaiting the start of the annual Medway Barge Race.

TO MAKE CLOUDS PAT SKY WASH with TISSUE, wet

1963 'Moonlight at Mersea'. Oil
20 × 30in

The moonlight scene at West Me
actually taken from a sketch don
daytime but converted into a moo
in order to evoke the quiet pleasu
on a calm night.

1976 Menai Straits: boats hauled u
Watercolour 10 × 15in

The watercolour and gouache pain
Menai Straits catches a transitory
as a gleam of sunshine sweeps over
It was painted on a hard, rough de V
oatmeal-tinted paper.

1976 Stangate Creek. Watercolour in the manner of Jan van de Cappelle 15 × 20in

The Stangate Creek sketch is an exercise, on a favourite theme, in the tradition of Dutch marine painting. It is one of several that Hilder has done of barges and other craft anchored in Stangate Creek, in the Medway, which is a safe deep water anchorage much used by commercial craft waiting for a tide to take them up to Rochester.

1969 'Birdham Pool, moonlight'. Watercolour 7 × 10in

When Rowland Hilder started drawing the Thames-side shipping at the beginning of the 1920s, there were no Turners, Whistlers or Monets at work. W. L. Wyllie was still painting down at Portsmouth and Frank Brangwyn was at the height of his fame. Popular marine painters of the time, such as Norman Wilkinson, Frank H. Mason, Charles Dixon, Montague Dawson and Charles Pears, were artists whose work was more often seen in reproduction and on the poster hoardings than in West End galleries. Outside England, the only European artist of note to be engaged in marine painting to any extent was Raoul Dufy, whose work today looks somewhat lightweight.

At that time Rowland Hilder, barely twenty years old, was spending every available moment drawing the shipping on the Thames, or sailing small boats, or taking steam trips round the coast. The result of this involvement, as we have seen, resulted in commissions to illustrate sea stories. He was already superbly

1970 'Evening on the Arun'. Watercolour 15 × 20in

equipped for this work, by his innate drawing ability, by his
experience afloat, by his knowledge of the tides and the shape of
the sea, and by the time he had spent in the Science Museum,
studying the details of hull and rigging in every kind of craft. But it
took more than this to make him a marine painter. He slowly
evolved methods of painting choppy seas and breaking waves, but
his real interest was in painting the quiet waters of estuaries and
tranquil harbours.

The Birdham Pool oil painting is based on various studies and of a
memory that the artist had of once anchoring there and of rowing
his dinghy through the mill pool on a night of a full moon.

This low-toned watercolour of the Arun river, with Arundel Castle
in the background, was done from sketches made on the deck of a
hired motor boat.

1975 Queenborough, Inner Harbour. Oil on canvas 28 × 40in

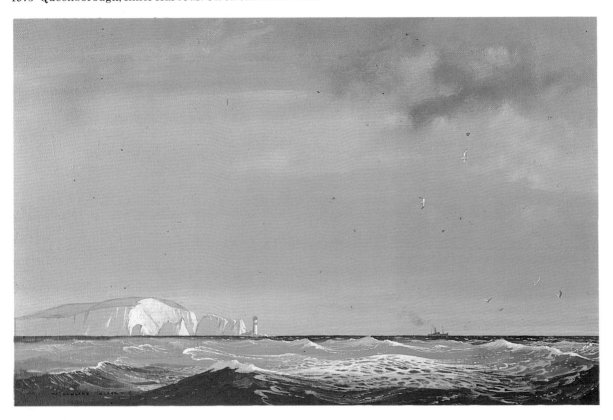

1962 The Needles. Oil on canvas 24 × 36in

154

1962 'Night at sea'. Watercolour and gouache 16½ × 30in

It was at this stage in his development that Hilder started studying Turner and backwards (chronologically) at that. From doing studies after Turner, such as *Windy Day* (page 113), he then looked at the earlier, Dutch-influenced Turner paintings. From these he worked his way backwards through Peter Monamy to Jan van de Cappelle. From the paintings of these artists he slowly forged a style that served him for pictures as different as the *Limehouse Reach* paintings on pages 158 and 159 and *Boats at Sète* and *Chioggia* on pages 162 and 163. His oil paintings, with their acrylic underpainting, became more defined and the watercolour sketches freer and more fluid.

This quite large watercolour and gouache painting was done in 1962 just after Rowland Hilder and his son Anthony had made a night crossing from Cherbourg to the Hamble river in their Atlanta sloop. It was apparently one of those nights to remember with a Force 4 wind on their quarter, a full moon and only the scantiest of cirrus clouds. The gouache body colour is painted on top of the watercolour washes to bring out the crests of the waves and the spume.

The painting of the inner harbour at Queenborough is a low tide picture. The oil painting on canvas was done from various sketches, made while staying at his coastguard cottage at Shellness. Queenborough is the nearest paintable place to Shellness. Hilder has used an acrylic underpainting in this picture as he has done in many others.

In the painting of the Needles, the seas breaking over shingle banks and the khaki colour of the shallow water is typical of the Solent on a windy day and even more so of the North Sea. Incidentally, the artist remarked that this viewpoint is taken from a point where no boat should be for these are dangerous and shallow waters!

Marine painting as we know it had its origins in Holland in the seventeenth century. It was introduced into England by the Dutch, particularly by the Willem van de Veldes, father and son. The Van de Veldes in fact established an English school of marine painting when they came to England in 1672. The younger Van de Velde in particular painted ships in the open sea from his personal experience. There was another Dutch marine painter who made almost as much impression and that was Jan van de Cappelle. He was a painter of tranquil estuary scenes and was a lasting influence on English painters like Charles Brooking, Peter Monamy and Samuel Scott.

This Dutch tradition was carried on by Turner in his early works – he even painted pastiche Dutch sea pieces – but later in the 1830s he abandoned this style in such paintings as *Keelmen heaving coals by night* or *Snowstorm: steam-boat off a harbour's mouth* which he painted in 1842. The old tradition however survived the impact of Turner's foretaste of Impressionism in the work of artists such as Clarkson Stanfield and E. W. Cooke.

It was Whistler who next brought new attitudes into English marine painting, with his atmospheric studies of the river Thames, so the arrival of Claude Monet in London in 1871 caused less of a furore than it might have done. After Turner, even the marine paintings of Monet, the greatest of the Impressionists, did not seem so outlandish. The lasting effects of Impressionism on English sea painting were minimal. Wilson Steer, with his Suffolk beach scenes, was almost the only English marine artist to have learnt anything from this movement.

It was to Whistler the etcher, rather than Whistler the painter that Hilder turned for inspiration. Whistler had settled in London in 1859 in a house overlooking the Thames and immediately started work on etchings of the river. The 'Thames Set' was exhibited at the Royal Academy in the following year. Etchings in this set such as 'Thames Police' or 'Black Lion Wharf' are a wonderful revelation of what London's waterside was like in the 1860s. It was these superb etchings that inspired Rowland Hilder, as a very young man, to sail up from Greenwich, in his search for subject matter, and to explore the wharves and basins of the Surrey Docks, Rotherhithe and Limehouse Reach.

The sketch at the top of the page opposite is of Hilder's favourite sailing ground. It is a view of the river Oare and the Shipwright's Arms, an old clapboard building where it is said that Turner once stayed. The pen drawing below is of the coastguard cottages on the other side of the Swale where Hilder has a studio.

1976 The River Oare and the Shipwrights'
Arms, based on sketches done in the 1930s.
$5 \times 6\frac{1}{4}$ in

1975 The Coastguard cottages at Shellness on
the Isle of Sheppey 2×6 in

1975 *Limehouse Reach*. Watercolour No 2. 11 × 16in

These paintings on the Limehouse Reach theme might be considered romantic evocations of the days of sail. In fact they are based on the actual memories that Hilder has of the Limehouse waterfront in years after the First World War when there were still Baltic timber brigs and Captain Erikson's great four-masted barques moored in the Thames. It was indeed the end of an era but Hilder was fortunate enough to be there to see it. The fact that he returns to the scenes of his youth for a series of paintings like these is not so very strange.

All three of these pictures are of virtually the same scene, but with changes of scale as he sought to find the most satisfactory composition. The low sun of the early morning remains constant in each picture. A dramatic side lighting effect has been a common factor in much of Hilder's work, though latterly he has taken to painting *contre jour*, that is, into the sun, with some success in such paintings as the two watercolours of the Isle of Sheppey on page 145.

1975 *Limehouse Reach No 1.* Oil on canvas 24 × 36in

1975 Limehouse Reach. Watercolour No 3
$7\frac{1}{4} \times 10\frac{1}{4}$in

1950 Greenwich Yacht Club. Watercolour 20 × 30in

The watercolour of Greenwich Yacht Club, of which Hilder has long been a member, was drawn on the spot. The picture was about 15 × 20in, as large a watercolour as one could comfortably do on a windy waterfront.

The watercolour sketch on the opposite page of the topsail schooner alongside a farm landing is based on drawings that the artist has done of numerous similar landing places in the East Anglian and north Kent estuaries. The square-rigger is a bit of nostalgic fancy, though it evokes John Ruskin's words in his Preface to Turner's *The Harbours of England*. 'Next to the fishing boat, ranks in interest to me the small, over-wrought, under-crewed, ill-caulked merchant schooner; the kind of ship which first shows its couple of thin masts over the low fields or marshes as we near any third-rate seaport.' Today it would be yachts, yesterday trading barges, but in the early years of the century it would have been the small over-wrought schooners or under-crewed brigs.

The view of the river Swale at low water is from Queenborough. The barge has just come through the swing bridge and is turning up to its anchorage. The painting is in watercolour, with body colour used for the whites; the blacks are put in with a felt pen and the fine lines with carbon pencil.

In 1960 the Hilders visited the Camargue. On one still afternoon they drove west to Sète and sat on the bank of the Canal de Mediterranée. There was a heat haze on the water which was as

1975   Nostalgic memory of riverside scene. Watercolour $7\frac{1}{4} \times 10\frac{1}{4}$in

1976 The Swale. Watercolour 10×15in

1972 Moored fishing boats, Sète. Oil on canvas 24 × 36in

smooth as polished marble. Just in front of them were three open boats, dory-like in the simplicity of their construction and a small fishing boat, painted blue with a red stripe, the colours as faded as an old pair of jeans. The tide, with almost imperceptible movement, was bringing down some flotsam of cut reeds and other rubbish. The feeling was one of complete tranquillity. They sat there for some hours, fascinated by the scene. The image of it stuck in Hilder's mind.

Not long after that they went to Venice and crossed the lagoon to Chioggia. This image of small craft resting on their mirrored reflections in smooth water was repeated. A trot of fishing boats was tied fore and aft between some piles. Once in a while they would gently swing to the scope of their warps. A dead leaf or a scrap of paper would float past. The heat haze and the invisible horizon was repeated. It was as if these craft had been abandoned to float in space. The feeling of tranquillity was again just as strong.

When Hilder came to paint these scenes at Sète and Chioggia, he turned to the use of oil paint, and to achieve the even tones of the merged sea and sky, he used acrylic paints for the underpainting. This method, used by contemporary artists as different as Hockney or Wyeth, provided him with the perfect medium for such subjects.

1973 Moored fishing boats, Chioggia. Oil on canvas 24 × 36in

1973 Small tugboat in creek, Hollow Shore, Faversham. Oil on canvas 24 × 36in

1975 'Turn of the Tide.' Oil on canvas 24 × 36in

1946 Rye Harbour: low water. Watercolour $7\frac{1}{4} \times 10\frac{1}{2}$in

1960 Study for painting of the Banffshire port of Macduff. Watercolour
$7\frac{1}{2} \times 10\frac{1}{4}$ in

The painting of the river Swale looking downstream from
Queenborough is called 'The turn of the tide'. One can see by the
ripples round the buoy in the foreground that the ebb has just set
in. This is one of Rowland Hilder's rare paintings of high water.
When he is staying at his coastguard cottage at Shellness, if the
tide is up and unless a full gale is blowing, he is out sailing in one of
his boats. He sails maybe for an hour or so either side of high water,
then he comes ashore and almost immediately goes out with his
sketch-book. As the tide recedes there is something infinitely
picturesque in the sight of glistening mudbanks, with small waders
running about by the tide line, and the river or creek confined to
narrow and tortuous channels. It would seem that he gets the best
of both worlds.

The sketch of boats at low water in Rye Harbour consists of a
series of short-hand notes that read most convincingly because of
the artist's complete understanding of the structure of a boat and
how it lies both in and out of the water.

The Moray Firth can be a bleak and stormy place but there are a
number of snug harbours, some large like Fraserburgh or Buckie
and some quite small like Burghead or Macduff. This watercolour
of Macduff was done in 1960 as a study for a painting. It is a free yet
assertive statement and provided a very adequate basis for the
final work.

1968 Harlow Mill. Watercolour 10 × 15in

1975 Hambledon Mill. Oil on canvas 24 × 36in

1975 Study of a pond. Watercolour $8\frac{3}{4} \times 12\frac{1}{2}$in

Hilder's marine paintings as often as not are of harbour scenes.
The transition to mill pools and inland lakes is an effortless one.
He likes painting water and he likes drawing buildings.

The watercolour of Harlow Mill was painted from a pre-war sketch
which Hilder had made whilst leaning over the parapet of a bridge.
Like several of the buildings that he has painted, this mill was
subsequently burnt down. He did an earlier version of this
watercolour in oils and it was exhibited at the Royal Academy in
the late 1930s. In a blistering review of that Summer Academy
Exhibition, the artist Wyndham Lewis said rather cryptically that
Hilder's painting of Harlow Mill was the only picture worth
looking at in the whole exhibition.

The painting of Hambledon Mill is in oil on canvas. It makes an
interesting comparison with the watercolour of Harlow Mill. By
this time Hilder's handling of oil paint had become very assured.
This competence was in part due to his having solved the problem
of underpainting, by the use of acrylic colours.

The watercolour (above) of the pond is taken from one of his
sketch-books. It is an effective and simple tonal study with the
trees and the punt and the landing stage in the foreground painted
in very broadly. Such an assured statement does depend on a
background of careful study.

1975 Canterbury. Watercolour 15 × 20in

1974 Staithes, Yorkshire. Watercolour 15 × 20in

1964 Wenlock Basin. Watercolour drawing on de Wint paper 15 × 20in

ARCHITECTURAL SUBJECTS

The architectural drawings on these pages show another aspect of
Rowland Hilder's work. The watercolour of Canterbury was
painted from the roof of the Odeon Cinema and shows one of the
few parts of this cathedral town that has not been destroyed by
bombs or wrecked by the developers.

The watercolour of Staithes was painted from notes made on the
spot. The artist was so beset by a flock of hungry seagulls, that any
serious outside work finally became quite impossible. Whilst
Hilder was making these studies, a heavy sea wrack moved in,
completely obliterating the town.

The watercolour drawing of Wenlock Basin was done on de Wint
paper from the roof of Royle Publications building in Wenlock
Road (just off the City Road). Wenlock Basin is an off-shoot of the
Grand Union Canal. At the end of the basin is Royle's printing
works.

1976 'Cast shadows'. Watercolour $9\frac{1}{4} \times 13$in

Hilder has always been a superb draughtsman, but this fact has been obscured by the kind of popular painting he has done, particularly his winter landscapes which were reproduced in their thousands. Between the 1930s and the 1960s there can have been few young married couples in England who could not boast of having a Rowland Hilder in their front room. It was no mean achievement to have given such widespread pleasure.

What is possibly a greater achievement is that he has managed to lift his work out of what was in danger of degenerating into a series of facile clichés. Once the pressure of working for advertising and reproduction were lifted, he applied himself to the real business of painting. The work speaks for itself.

1968 Study of trees. Pen and ink $7\frac{1}{2} \times 6$in

This study of winter trees makes an appropriate tailpiece to this
book about Rowland Hilder. Winter trees are still one of the
recurring themes in his work. They date from his illustrations in
Precious Bane, which were based on drawings of the November
landscape of Shropshire in 1928. These were drawn in pen and ink,
as is this study which was used on a gallery card for an exhibition
of his work at the Furneaux Gallery in 1968.

Books illustrated by Rowland Hilder

The Riddle of the Air Percy F. Westerman Blackie 1925

Moby Dick Herman Melville Jonathan Cape 1926

The Adventures of a Trafalgar Lad John Lesterman Jonathan
Cape 1926

The Junior Cadet Percy F. Westerman Blackie 1927

A Sailor of Napoleon John Lesterman Jonathan Cape 1927

A Pair of Rovers John Lesterman Jonathan Cape 1928
(Illustrated in collaboration with Richard Southern)

The Second Mate of the Myradale John Lesterman Jonathan
Cape 1929

Treasure Island R. L. Stevenson Oxford University Press 1929

Then and Now Shell Mex Ltd 1929

Precious Bane Mary Webb Jonathan Cape 1929

Kidnapped R. L. Stevenson Oxford University Press 1930

The Senior Cadet Percy F. Westerman Blackie 1931

Little Peter the Great H. A. Manhood Jackson 1931

The Midnight Folk John Masefield Heinemann 1931

True Tales of the Sea C. Fox-Smith Oxford University Press 1932

In Defence of British Rivers Shell Mex and BP Ltd 1932

Fire Down Below W. M. W. Watt Müller 1935

They went to the Island L. A. G. Strong Dent 1940

The Bible for Today Ed. John Stirling Oxford University Press 1941
(Illustrated in collaboration with other artists)

The Shell Guide to Flowers of the Countryside Geoffrey Grigson
Phoenix House 1955
(Illustrated in collaboration with Edith Hilder)

Starting with Watercolour written and illustrated by Rowland
Hilder Studio Vista 1966

Index